FENG-SHUI

3 ⁰⁰
08-20

FENG-SHUI

ERNEST J. EITEL

commentary by John Michell

Graham Brash, Singapore

Reprinted 1985, 1987, 1990, 1993, 1995, 1997 by
Graham Brash (Pte) Ltd
85, Genting Lane, #05-01
Singapore 349569

ISBN 981-218-037-0

Illustration by THOMAS ALLOM from
China Illustrated, 1843
Printed in Singapore by KHL Printing Co. Pte. Ltd.

CONTENTS

FOREWORD by John Michell

AFTERWORD by John Michell

Concise Bibliography on Feng-Shui

*A late Chhing representation of the selection of a city site;
the geomancer is consulting his magnetic compass.*

FOREWORD

This is the third edition of Eitel's classic work since 1973, the centenary of its first printing. Interest in feng-shui has developed strongly in Europe and America during the last decade, and the fact that many copies of the previous edition of this book were sold in Taiwan, Hong Kong and elsewhere in the East is one indication of the current revival of feng shui in its native territories. The reasons for its new popularity seem to be two-fold. The first, and naturally the most widely appreciated, is the legendary ability of the feng-shui practitioners to bring good luck to their clients through their esoteric methods of adjusting the arrangements of their domestic or business premises. Numerous anecdotes, both ancient and modern, testify to the efficacy of feng-shui in attracting fortune and averting calamities. Typical is that of the house which seemed always to bring bad luck to its tenants. No one felt truly at ease it it. New owners (having bought it cheap) called in the feng-shui man, who diagnosed the cause of its disturbed atmosphere. It may have been due to underground waters, the influence of a nearby tall building (casting 'secret arrows'), a narrow street pointing directly at the house or some awkwardness in its internal arrangements. Whatever were the sources of trouble, the feng-shui man was able to counteract them by his knowledge and techniques, deflecting evil forces by mirrors, altering or moving the front door or redesigning the interior. The effect in any case was to change the atmosphere of the house and bring contentment and profit to its owners.

A story of this type, though with an unhappy ending, is told about the late kung-fu star, Bruce Lee, whose sudden death is attributed by his compatriots to his carelessness over feng-shui. It is said that the house he lived in had been notoriously unlucky until a feng-shui man was engaged to put things right. This he did, expensively, mainly by means of a feng-shui structure on the roof. The device fell or was knocked down, Bruce Lee neglected to replace it and his death came shortly afterwards.

The second reason for feng-shui's modern revival leads directly to the heart of the subject. In China up to the present century feng-shui was an official state science, directed by the Board of Rites in Peking and patronized by the Emperor himself. In its heydey, when it was practised for public benefit and not only for private individuals, it produced that great artistic masterpiece, the classic Chinese landscape, highly populous and productive yet so delightfully laid out and ornamented that travellers compared it to a continuous landscape-garden. The harmonious aspect and atmosphere of old China were created by the feng-shui men with their mysterious science. It is that achievement and the lessons to be learned from it which are now attracting architects, planners and others who are concerned about the relationship of human societies to our natural surroundings to investigate the aims and methods of feng-shui.

The Rev. E.J. Eitel of the London Missionary Society took good advantage of his posting to China by studying and writing about Buddhism and made his name as the first European authority on feng-shui. Not only was he meticulous in describing details of the old science, he was also able to enter into the spirit of it, convey something of that to his readers and even admit grudging admiration for some of its aspects. But clearly he was in two minds about his subject, whether it pertained to God or the Devil, and in the first and last paragraphs of this book he asks himself or his readers the question which constantly puzzled him: What is feng-shui?

Various answers to this question have been offered by writers since Eitel's day. Ernst Börschmann in his book on the old Chinese landscape, *Picturesque China*, wrote:

"This well known word (feng-shui) means wind-water, but in its wider sense stands for the relations to the surrounding nature, the influence of the landscape on the beauty of the buildings and the happiness of the inhabitants."

A modern writer on feng-shui, Stephen Skinner, describes it thus:

"The art of living in harmony with the land, and deriving the greatest benefit, peace and prosperity from being in the right place at the right time is called feng-shui."

A third, traditional definition of feng-shui is "The art of adapting the residences of the living and the dead so as to co-operate and harmonize with the local currents of the cosmic breath".

Börschmann, a German photographer who worked in China in the early years of this century and published in his book some haunting pictures of its feng-shui monuments, was one of the first of his generation to express sympathetic appreciation of it. The sacred landscape of China, he wrote, is designed around its five mountains, four at the cardinal points and one at the centre, in such a way that the whole country can be regarded as one great temple precinct. On the works of the feng-shui men he wrote:

"Certain summits...are crowned with pagodas, small temples or pagodas to harmonize the magic forces of heaven and earth. This thought is akin, for instance, to our conception of the putflow of magnetic force from a pointed conductor. And the Chinese geomancer (feng-shui man) also regards the forms of nature as a magnetic field."

Joseph Needham in *Science and Civilization in China* concisely describes the function of feng-shui.

"Every place had its special topographical features which modified the local influence of the various ch'i (energies) of Nature. The forms of hills and the directions of watercourses, being the outcome of the moulding influences of winds and waters, were the most important, but, in addition, the heights and forms of buildings, and the directions of roads and bridges, were potent factors. The force and nature of the invisible currents would be from hour to hour modified by the positions of the heavenly bodies, so their aspects as seen from the locality in question had to be considered. While the choosing of sites was of prime importance, bad siting was not irremediable, as ditches and tunnels could be dug, or other measures taken to alter the feng-shui situation..."

To the credit of feng-shui, according to Needham, is "the great beauty of the siting of so many farms, houses and villages throughout China".

It is the phenomenon referred to in the above accounts as 'cosmic breath', 'magic forces', 'ch'i' and 'invisible currents' which has made feng-shui such a mystery to western understanding. All who have written about it agree that feng-shui recognizes, besides the palpable elements such as wind and water, certain types of energy which permeate the earth and atmosphere and animate the forms of nature; but further understanding has been blocked by the impossibility of equating these energies with phenomena recognized by modern physics. In one aspect they evidently correspond to the emanations from the earth which are detected by water-diviners, or to the earth's magnetic currents. Sometimes they seem purely aesthetic and psychological, as expressing one's feelings of unease in ugly, ill-proportioned surroundings and the soothing effect of a beautiful building or landscape. At other times they are personified as genii loci, the nature gods, fairies and spirits of the dead which haunt the countryside and its natural shrines. Whereas the modern tendency is to separate these energies and concepts into different categories, the Chinese regarded the invisible side of nature as a whole, and formulated in feng-shui a code of practice to govern their relations to it. The geological, atmospheric and psychic qualities of every potential building site were assessed together by the one science, which determined the position and planning of all houses and types of construction throughout China.

According to the traditional histories of China, art and science were discovered by the first ruler, Fu Hsi, who, "looking upwards contemplated the images in the heavens, and looking downwards observed the patterns on the earth". Thus he gained insight into the laws of nature and the influence of cosmic forces on all life below. In his wisdom he instituted feng-shui to sanctify the lives of his people, attune them to the moods and rhythms of nature and provide them with security and a sense of continuity. At certain intervals in history the cosmology which is at the root of feng-shui and other traditional sciences has been disputed or neglected, but such periods have always been followed by its revival and a renaissance of culture. The lesson of long experience is that the way of thought associated with feng-shui comes closer than any other reflecting the natural human mentality and the reality of our situation on earth. It is therefore as inevitable as tomorrow's sunrise that this way of thought will once more prevail and that feng-shui, in one form or another, will contribute to the science of the future. It is that prospect (further discussed in the *Afterword* following Eitel's treatise) which is generating such intense modern interest in the old Chinese science of landscape.

What is Feng-shui? This is a question which has been asked over and over again for the last thirty years. Ever since foreigners were allowed to settle down on the confines of this strange empire of China, this same question has been cropping up continually here and there. When purchasing a site, when building a house, when pulling down a wall, or raising a flagstaff—residents in the Treaty Ports have encountered innumerable difficulties, and all on account of Feng-shui. When it was proposed to erect a few telegraph poles, when the construction of a railway was urged upon the Chinese Government, when a mere tramway was suggested to utilize the coal-mines of the interior. Chinese officials would invariably make a polite bow and declare the thing impossible on account of Feng-shui. When, thirty years ago, the leading merchants of the Colony of Hongkong endeavoured to place the business part of the town in the so-called Happy Valley, and to make that part of the island the centre of the whole town, they ignominiously failed on account of Feng-shui. When the Hongkong Government cut a road, now known as the Gap, to the Happy Valley, the Chinese community was thrown into a state of abject terror and fright, on account of

A legendary spot in the Woo-tang mountains adorned with feng-shui monuments.

the disturbance which this amputation of the dragon's limbs would cause to the Feng-shui of Hongkong; and when many of the engineers, employed at the cutting, died of Hongkong fever, and the foreign houses already built in the Happy Valley had to be deserted on account of malaria, the Chinese triumphantly declared, it was an act of retributory justice on the part of Feng-shui. When Senhor Amaral, the Governor of Macao, who combined with a great passion for constructing roads an unlimited contempt for Feng-shui, interfered with the situation and aspects of Chinese tombs, he was waylaid by Chinese, his head cut off, and the Chinese called this dastardly deed the revenge of Feng-shui.

Surely there must be something in Feng-shui, if it drives the lowest classes of Chinese to commit a foul murder, and is eagerly availed of by ministers of state as a satisfactory excuse for their own unwillingness to further the progress of trade and civilisation.

What is Feng-shui? Sinologues looked through the Chinese Classics for an answer to this question, searched through their Dictionaries, and found none. Merchants asked their compradores and house-boys, What is Feng-shui? but the replies they got were rather obscure and confused, and at best they were told, that Feng-shui means "wind and water," and is so called, "because it's a thing like wind, which you cannot comprehend, and like water, which you cannot grasp."

But, strange to say, Chinese constantly assert, that foreigners know all about Feng-shui. When mortality was frightful among the Hongkong troops quartered in Murray Barracks, and the Colonial Surgeon proposed the planting of bamboos at the back of the buildings, the Chinese justly remarked, that this measure was in strict accordance with Feng-shui; and when it was found, that disease was actually checked thereby, they looked upon it as a proof of the virtues of Feng-shui. When foreign residents of Hongkong began to build villas in Pok-foo-lum (which Feng-shui declares to be the best site of the island), when the Government began to build a reservoir there, when tanks were built on the north side of Hongkong, and the hill-side studded with trees, when the cutting of earth was forbidden in places where there is much decomposed rock, the Chinese in all these cases supposed foreigners to know more about Feng-shui than they would tell, and the Surveyor General was put down as a profound adept in Feng-shui. Why, they say, there is Government House, occupying the very best spot on the northern side of the island, screened at the back by high trees and gently-shelving terraces, skirted right and left by roads with graceful curves, and the whole situation combining everything that Feng-shui would prescribe—how is it possible that foreigners pretend to know nothing of Feng-shui?

Well, if Feng-shui were no more than what our common sense and natural instincts teach us, Chinese Feng-shui would be no such puzzle to us. But the fact is, the Chinese have made Feng-shui a black art, and those that are proficient in this art and derive their livelihood from it, find it to their advantage to make the same mystery of it, with which European alchemists and astrologers used to surround their vagaries. Every resident of China, however, acquires by a few years' practical intercourse with the Chinese a tolerably clear idea of what Feng-shui is, and most of my readers no doubt know, that practically speaking it is simply a system of super-stition, supposed to teach people where and when to build a tomb or to erect a house so as to insure for those concerned everlasting prosperity and happiness.

Since my arrival in China I have had a great many practical collisions with Feng-shui, and having for many years collected notes on the subject and studied its literature in all its branches, I now propose to lay the result of my studies before the public. Feng-shui is however, as I take it, but another name for natural science; and I must ask therefore the indulgence of my readers, for my introducing a general outline of Chinese physical science in order to make the system of Feng-shui intelligble.

4.

Natural science has never been cultivated in China in that technical, dry and matter-of-fact fashion, which seems to us inseparable from true science. Chinese naturalists did not take much pains in studying nature and ferreting out her hidden secrets by minute and practical tests and experiments. They invented no instruments to aid them in the observation of the heavenly bodies, they never took to hunting beetles and stuffing birds, they shrank from the idea of dissecting animal bodies, nor did they chemically analyse inorganic substances, but with very little actual knowledge of nature they evolved a whole system of natural science from their own inner consciousness and expounded it according to the dogmatic formulæ of ancient tradition. Deplorable, however, as this absence of practical and experimental investigation is, which opened the door to all sorts of conjectural theories, it preserved in Chinese natural science a spirit of sacred reverence for the divine powers of nature.

Though modern Confucianism has long ago discarded the belief in one supreme personal God, of which their classical writings still preserve a dead record, and though they substituted, for the personal God whom their forefathers worshipped, an abstract entity, devoid of personality, devoid of all attributes whatsoever, yet they look upon nature not as a dead inanimate fabric, but as a living breathing organism. They see a golden chain of spiritual life running through every form of existence and binding together, as in one living body, everything that subsists in heaven above or on earth below. What has so often been admired in the natural philosophy of the Greeks—that they made nature live; that they saw in every stone, in every tree, a living spirit; that they peopled the sea with naiads, the forests with satyrs—this poetical, emotional and reverential way of looking at natural objects, is equally so a characteristic of natural science in China.

The whole system of Feng-shui is based on this emotional conception of nature. We may smile at the unscientific, rudimentary character of Chinese physiology; we may point out, that every branch of science in China is but a rudimentary groping after truths with which every school-boy in Europe is familiar; we may conclude, that China as a whole resembles but an over-grown child, on whose intellect has fallen a sudden blight and who grew up since to manhood, to old age, with no more knowledge than that of a precocious baby; and yet I saw, looking at this same China, the oldest among ancient peoples, the greatest among great empires, or at least the most populous among all the countries of the world, hoary with old age, heavy, dull, childishly ignorant as regards matters of intellect—yet I say, would God, that our own men of science had preserved in their observatories, laboratories and lecture-rooms that same child-like reverence for the living powers of nature, that sacred awe and trembling fear of the mysteries of the unseen, that firm belief in the reality of the invisible world and its constant intercommunication with the seen and the temporal, which characterise these Chinese gropings after natural science.

The system of Feng-shui is of comparatively modern origin. Its diagrams and leading ideas are indeed borrowed from one of the ancient classics, but its method and practical application are almost wholly based on the teachings of Choo-he and others, who lived under the Sung dynasty (A.D. 1126-1278), and whose commentaries to the classics are read in every school. Choo-he's mode of thinking has in fact been adopted by modern Confucianism, and forms the philosophical basis of the whole system of Feng-shui.

According to Choo-he there was in the beginning one abstract principle or monad, called the "absolute nothing", which evolved out of itself the "great absolute". This abstract principle or monad, the great absolute, is the primordial cause of all existence. When it first moved, its breath or vital energy congealing, produced the great male principle. When it had moved to the uttermost it rested, and in resting produced the female principle. After it had rested to the utmost extent, it again moved, and thus went on in alternate motion and rest without cessation. When this supreme cause thus divided itself into male and female, that which was above constituted heaven, and that which was beneath formed the earth. Thus it was that heaven and earth were made. But the supreme cause having produced by evolution the male and female principles, and through them heaven and earth, ceased not its constant permutations, in the course of which men and animals, vegetables and minerals, rose into being. The same vital energy, moreover, continued to act ever since, and continued to act through those two originating causes, the male and female powers of nature, which ever since mutually and alternately push and agitate one another, without a moment's intermission.

Now, the energy animating the two principles is called in Chinese Hi, or the breath of nature. When this breath first went forth and produced the male and female principles and finally the whole universe, it did not do so arbitrarily or at random, but followed fixed, inscrutable and immutable laws. These laws or order of nature, called Li, were therefore abstractly considered prior to the issuing of the vital breath, and must therefore be considered separately. Again, considering this Li, or the general order of the universe, the ancient sages observed that all the laws of nature and all the workings of its vital breath are in strict accordance with certain mathematical principles, which may be traced and illustrated by diagrams, exhibiting the numerical proportion of the universe called So, or numbers. But the breath of nature or the Hi, the order of nature called Li, and the mathematical proportions of nature, called So, these three principles are not directly cognizable to the senses, they are hidden from view, and only become manifest through forms and outlines of physical nature. In other words, the phenomena of nature, her outward forms of appearance, constitute a fourth branch of the system of natural science called Ying, or forms of nature. Now these four divisions, Li, or the general order of nature,

So, her numerical proportions, Hi, her vital breath or subtle energies, and Ying, her forms of appearance, constitute what is popularly called the system of Feng-shui.

No Chinese work on Feng-shui, however—or at least none that I have seen or heard of—follows out this division methodically, though they all mention these four principles and give them here and there due prominence. On the other hand, this division of four branches of the Feng-shui system is not my own. A distinguished Cantonese scholar, a member of the Imperial College, mentions, in a preface which he wrote to a popular geomantic work, that the whole system of Feng-shui might advantageously be divided into the above-mentioned four parts. From this preface I have taken the hint, and propose now to set before my readers the system of Feng-shui, following out this fourfold plan, and working it out so that it should give them an insight into the whole system of Chinese natural science generally.

In accordance with the foregoing remarks, I have to deal first with Li, or the general principles ruling nature, with the laws of the physical universe. To understand these aright we must at the outset keep in mind, that the Chinese look upon heaven as the ideal type, of which our earth is but the coarse material reflex.

Everything that exists on earth is but the transient form of appearance of some celestial agency. Everything terrestrial has its prototype, its primordial cause, its ruling agency in heaven. The Chinese philosopher, looking at the beauties of nature, the variety of hills and plains, rivers and oceans, the wonderful harmony of colour, light and shade, sees in it but the dim reflex of that more splendid scenery frescoed in ethereal beauty on heaven's starry firmament. He gazes at the sun, that dazzling regent of the day, and recognizes in him, as his terrestrial reflex, the male principle of creation, ruling everything that is under the sun. He lifts up his eye to the moon, the beautiful queen of the night, and sees her reflex on earth in the female principle, pervading all sublunary forms of existence. He observes the swift rotatory course of the five planets, Jupiter, Mars, Venus, Mercury and Saturn,

The Fortress of Terror, Ting-hai, Chusan, in a rich feng-shui landscape with farm-house and octagonal Hall of Ancestors.

and sees their counterpart on earth in the ceaseless interchange and permutations of the five elements of nature, wood, fire, metal, water and earth. He contemplates the spangled firmament at night, and compares with its dimly-reflected transcript on the surface of our earth, where the mountain peaks form the stars, the rivers and oceans answer to the milky way.

In short, the firmament of heaven is to a Chinese beholder the mysterious text-book, in which the laws of nature, the destinies of nations, the fate and fortunes of every individual are written in hieroglyphic mystic characters, intelligible to none but to the initiated. Now, to decipher these tablets of heaven, to break the seals of this apocalyptic book, is the prime object of Feng-shui; and the first method to be employed in the deciphering of this heavenly horoscope of the future, the first key that is to be inserted to unlock that puzzling safe, in which the fortunes of present and future generations are locked up, is the knowledge of the general principles or laws of nature.

Learn then, if you will your fortunes, and treasure well these lessons: 1. That heaven rules the earth; 2. That both heaven and earth will influence all living beings and that it is in your hands to turn this influence to the best account for your advantage; 3. That the fortunes of the living depend also upon the goodwill and general influence of the dead.

As to the first point, the influence which heaven exercises upon the earth, the agencies that come under consideration here are the sun and the moon, with the twelve signs of the zodiac and the twenty-eight constellations, the five planets—for only five are known to the Chinese—seven stars of the Great Bear and nine other stars of the northern bushel.

The sun, as we have remarked before, influences the whole physical universe and the sun's apparent course, as marked by the twelve zodiacal signs, is therefore an important element in the calcualtion of heaven's influence upon earth.

The Chinese divide the ecliptic into twelve equal parts, to

each of which they give the name of some animal. Thus the first they call the rat; it corresponds to Aries. the next is called the ox, and it is our identical Taurus; the third, which they call the tiger, corresponds to Gemini; the fourth, or the hare, corresponds to Cancer; the fifth, the dragon, answers to Leo; the sixth, or the snake, to Virgo; the seventh, called the horse, to Libra; the eighth, the ram, to Scorpio; the ninth, the monkey, to Sagittarius; the tenth, the cock, to Capricorn; the eleventh, the dog, to Aquarius; and the twelfth, the boar, to Pisces; Owing to the precession of the equinoxes or the shifting of the equinoctical points from east to west, a change has occurred—since the ancestors of the Chinese fixed upon these twelve asterisms—I say a change has occurred in the relations between the signs of the zodiac and their respective asterisms. Two thousand years ago the zodiacal signs and asterisms corresponded, so that when the sun entered the first point of the sign Aries, he entered also the constellation of the same name. The effect of the precession of the equinoxes has been to separate the asterisms from their denominational signs, so that the constellation Pisces is now in the sign Aries and the sign Aries is the sign Taurus. The Chinese, now knowing of the precession of the equinoxes, are rather perplexed by the discrepancy, but caring less for accuracy and more for ancient tradition, ignore the actual discrepancy, and still represent the twelve signs, not as they appear now, but as they appeared to their ancestors two thousand years ago. They use the twelve zodiacal signs especially to determine the twenty-four seasons of the year. When the sun enters the 15th degree of Aquarius (February 5th) spring begins. When he enters Pisces (February 19th) the rainy season sets in; when he reaches the 15th degree of Pisces (March 5th) insects get excited; when he enters Aries (March 30th) the vernal equinox comes round, followed (April 5th) by the term called "bright and clear"; entering Taurus (April 20th) he brings fructifying rain and (May 5th) the beginning of summer; in Gemini (May 21st) he brings the two terms called "the grain is filling" and (June 6th) "the grain is in the ear"; in Cancer he brings the two terms summer solstice (June 21st) and little heat (July 7th); when the sun is in Leo (June 23rd) the great heat begins and (August 7th) autumn sets in; when the sun is in Virgo (August 23rd) heat is limited and (September 8th) white dew will fall; when the sun is in Libra (September 23rd) the autumnal equinox takes place and (October 8th) cold dew descends; when in Scorpio (October 23rd) frost falls and (November 7th) winter sets in; when in Sagittarius (November 22nd) little snow will fall, and (December 7th) great snow; when the sun is in Capricorn (December 22nd) the winter solstice takes place and (January 6th) little cold sets in; when the sun enters Aquarius (January 20th) great cold sets in; and thus the circle of the year is completed.

Next in importance to the twelve zodiacal signs come the twenty-eight constellations, or abodes, through which the moon travels in her monthly course along the ecliptic. These twenty-eight constellations are divided into four sections, one of which is called the azure dragon, located in the East, and comprising the first seven constellations. The next seven constellations are called the sable warrior, whose abode is in the North; the third seven bear the name of the white tiger; situated in the West, and the last seven are designated the vermilion bird, ruling the South. But besides these four constellations which are looked upon as spirits influencing the earth, it is further to be observed that of these twenty-eight constellations Numbers 4, 11, 18 and 25 form a lucky conjunction with the sun, Nos. 5, 12, 19 and 26 with the moon; whilst of the five planets the following conjunctions are luck-bringing, Jupiter with Nos. 1, 8, 15, 22, Venus with Nos. 2, 9, 16, 23, Saturn with Nos. 3, 10, 17 and 24, Mars with Nos. 6, 13, 21 and 27, and Mercury with Nos. 7, 14, 20 and 28.

Besides the twenty-eight constellations, the five planets known to the Chinese and the occult virtues ascribed to them play a very important part in the system of Feng-shui. Jupiter is said to reign in the East, ruling the spring and has the attribute of benevolence. Mars dwells in the South, commands the summer and favours propriety. Venus dwells in the West, rules in the autumn and her province is decorum. Mercury is located in the North, rules in winter and is the representative of wisdom. Saturn reigns in the middle of the earth, rules midsummer and is characterized by fidelity.

There are other heavenly bodies which likewise exercise an influence upon the earth. As the five planets form, in addition to the sun and moon, the seven rulers of the seasons, thus also the seven stars of the Great Bear contribute their quota to the direction of the seasons. This splendid constellation has attracted the attention and poetical fancy of almost every nation on earth; but I never heard of any people that turned this remarkable cluster of stars to such a practical account. The Chinese look upon the seven stars of the Great Bear as forming a natural clock. For the body of the Great Bear being in ancient times considerably nearer to the North Pole than it is now, the tail appeared to move round the pole somewhat like the hand of a clock or watch. Considering then the earth's surface to form the dial-plate and dividing the horizon into twenty-four equal parts, whilst the tail of the Great Bear acts as the hands of the clock, we have a simple method of determine the above mentioned twenty-four seasons of year. When the tail of the Great Bear points, at nightfall, to the East, it is spring to all the world. When it points to the South, it is summer; when it points to the West, it is autumn; and when it points, at nightfall, to the North, it is winter. The light of these seven stars is supposed moreover to exercise a great influence upon the earth and upon all dwellers on earth, and these seven stars are, therefore, combined with sun and moon, called the nine luminaries of the world.

There is another set of stars, called the nine stars of the bushel, which are likewise of great importance for the determination of lucky or unlucky aspects of any given locality and its consequent influence upon the fate of men. These nine stars are minutely described in every Chinese almanack or calendar, but it is difficult to determine their position on the sky. They are called "the nine stars of the northern bushel;" but the latter term is sometimes applied to the North Pole, sometimes to the Great Bear, sometimes to one of the twenty-eight constellations called the bushel. But their position in the heavens is of little importance—some authorities even say they have no fixed place at all, but are moving about in the atmosphere—for they have each and all their counterparts or representatives on earth in the shape of mountains, and it is the business and art of the geomancer to determine which mountain-peak or hill corresponds to the one or other of these nine stars, each, of which has its own permanent relation to one of the five elements or to one of the above-mentioned eight diagrams.

The next point to be considered is the influence which both heaven and earth exercise upon human beings. The principal agents through which heaven, and especially the five planets, act upon all living creatures are the five elements of nature. By these however we must not understand five material substances, chemically indissoluble, but rather spiritual essences, each characteristically different from the other and forming the generative causes of all material substances. These five elements are wood, fire, earth, metal and water, the first of them being the agent of Jupiter, the second that of Mars, the third that of Saturn, the fourth that of Venus, the fifth that of Mercury. But it is also important to observe the mutual relation of the five elements to each other, for they both produce and destroy each other if placed in certain conjunctions. Wood produces fire, fire produces earth, earth produces metal, metal produces water, water produces wood. On the other hand, metal destroys wood, wood destroys (i.e. absorbs) earth, earth destroys (i.e. absorbs) water, water destroys fire, fire destroys metal. Again it is to be considered that wood is abundant in the East, metal in the West, water in the North, fire in the South, whilst earth predominates in the centre between the four cardinal points. It is also to be borne in mind, that wood reigns in spring, fire in summer, metal in autumn, water in winter, aand earth during the last eighteen days of each season. In this way the fivefold influence of the planets pervades and rules all nature, as, for instance, the five constituents of the human frame, muscles, veins, flesh, bones, skin, and hair; the five inward parts of viscera, viz., heart, liver, stomach, lungs, and kidneys; the five colours, white, black, red, blue, and yellow; the five fortunes, riches, honour, longevity, children, and a peaceful death; the five social relations, prince and minister, father and son, husband and wife, older and younger brothers, and friends.

In addition to the influence which according to the laws of nature heaven and earth exercise upon the destinies of living beings, there are to be considered the laws regulating the influence of the spirits of the dead upon the living. This is a doctrine which seems strange to us, but which has nothing unreasonable in itself to a Chinaman accustomed to worship the spirits of his ancestors, whom he supposes to be constantly hovering near, and to whom he therefore formally announces every event in his family, and offers sacrifices of meat and drink. "My own animal spirits," says the Commentator of the Analects of Confucious, "are the animal spirits of my progenitors. When on my part I carry to the utmost my sincerity and respect in worshipping them, then the spirits of my ancestors are present with me. Just like a stalk of grain, when the original plant is dead, new roots appear on the side—thus connecting the identical real spirit down from past generations to the present time." Though we speak of heaven and earth, said Choo-he, yet there is in reality but one breath (spirit) that upholds them. Though we speak of individuals, and distinguish one from the other, yet there is in reality but one breath that animates them all. My own breath (spirit) is the identical breath (spirit) of my ancestors.

This idea of the organic unity, nay identity, of the spritual basis of live in nature and live in individuals, was a favourite theme of discussion with Choo-he and other philosophers of the Sung dynasty. According to this now universally influential school, the human soul is possessed of a dual nature, and leads, as it were, a double life. They distinguish an animus and an anima. The former is the energy of human nature as embodying the male principle of nature. The breath of the animus is the breath of heaven. The anima, on the other hand, is the redundancy or plethoma, so to speak, of the contracting (female) energy of nature. The breath of the anima is the breath of the earth. The animus is the spiritual, the anima the material or animal elemnet of the soul. When, through the exhaustion of the vital breath, the body is broken up, the animus returns to heaven, the anima to earth; that is to say, each is dissolved again into those general elements of nature whence each derived its origin and the temporary embodiment of which each was within the sphere of individual life. The souls of deceased ancestors therefore are as omnipresent as the elements of nature, as heaven and earth themselves. Thus the Chinese have been taught to consider themselves as constantly surrounded by a spirit world, invisible indeed and inaccessible by touch or handling, but none the less real, none the less influential.

Now, the common people have the notion, which is no doubt but a popularized application of the above-given philosophical propositions, that the souls of the ancestors are by their animal nature chained, as it were, for some time to the tomb in which their bodies are interred, whilst by their spiritual nature they feel impelled to hover near the dwellings of their descendants, whence it is but a natural and logical inference to suppose, that the fortunes of the living depend in some measure upon the favourable situation of the tombs of their ancestors. If a tomb is so placed, that the animal spirit of the deceased, supposed to dwell there, is comfortable and free of disturbing elements, so that the soul has un-restricted egress and ingress, the ancestors' spirits will feel well disposed towards their descendants, will be enabled to constantly surround them, and willing to shower upon them all the blessings within reach of the spirit world. So deeply ingrafted is this idea of the influence of the dead upon the living, that Chinese wishing to get into the good graces of foreigners will actually go out to the Hong-kong cemeteries in the Happy Valley, and worship there at the tombs of foreigners, supposing that the spirits of the dead there, pleased with their offerings and worship, would influence the spirits of the living, and thus produce a mutual good under-standing between all the parties concerned.

Naturally, therefore, every Chinaman takes the greatest pains to place the tombs of his relatives in such a situation, that no star or planet above, nor any terrestrial element below, no breath or subtle influence of nature, no ill-portending configuration of hills and dales, should disturb the quiet repose of the dead, for upon this depend the fortunes and misfortunes of the living. It is consequently important to know the rules by which the luckiest spot for a grave can be found, and as the place best adapted for a grave depends principally upon the happiest conjunction of all heavenly and terrestrial elements, it is clear, that the method by which the most suitable site for a tomb is found, is also applicable for the selection of a good site for a dwelling-house or any place of abode whatsoever. For the same influ-ences which act upon the animal spirits of the dead have also their bearing upon the living.

We have to do here, however, only with general principles, and I will state the rules applicable to this purpose as briefly as possible.

In the first instance it must be understood, that there are in the earth's crust two different, shall I say magnetic, currents, the one male, the other female; the one positive, the other negative; the one favourable, the other unfavourable.

The one is allegorically called the azure dragon, the other the white tiger. The azure dragon must always be to the left, the white tiger to the right of any place supposed to contain a luck-bringing site. This therefore is the first business of the geomancer on looking out for a propitious site, to find a true dragon, and its complement the white tiger, both being discernible by certain elevations of the ground. Dragon and tiger were constantly compared with the lower and upper portion of a man's arm: in the bend of the arm the favourable site must be looked for. In other words, in the angle formed by dragon and tiger, in the very point where the two (magnetic) currents which they individually represent cross each other, there may be the luck-bringing site, the place for a tomb or dwelling, be found. I say it *may* be found there, because, besides the conjunction of dragon and tiger, there must be there also a tranquil harmony of all the heavenly and terrestrial elements which influence that particular spot, and which is to be determined by observing the compass and its indication of the numerical proportions, and by examining the direction of the water courses.

In illustration of this I may remark that the favourable situation of Canton city consists in this, that it is placed in the very angle formed by two chains of hills running in gentle curves towards the Bogue, where they almost meet each other, forming a complete horse-shoe. The chain of hills known as the White Clouds represent the dragon, whilst the undulating ground of the other side of the river forms the white tiger. The most favourable site of Canton is therefore the ground near the North-gates, whence tiger and dragon run out to the right and left. For the luckiest spot, say the Feng-shui books, is like a modest virgin, loving retirement, and it is therefore one of the first rules to look in a doubtful case, for a happy site in a recess.

Another rule is, that on perfectly monotonous ground, on a perfectly level plain, or on monotonously steep declivities, where there is no indication of dragon and tiger, no good site can possibly be found.

A third rule is to observe the distinction of male and female ground. Boldly rising elevations are called male, whilst uneven, softly-undulating ground is called female ground. On ground where the male characteristics prevail, the lucky site is on a spot having female characteristics, either visible to to the eye or indicated by the compass, whilst on a locality which is to be classed on the whole among female ground, the spot for a grave or house should have indications of the male principle ruling there. But the most favourable prognostics belong to a spot where there is a transition from male to female or from female to male ground, and where the surroundings combine—as indicated by the compass—both male and female characteristics in the proper proportion, which the Feng-shui books state to be three-fifths male to two-fifths female ground. Where however the female indications exceed the male, there are malign influences, counteracting all other favaourable configuations.

Finally, the place to be chosen for a grave or a tomb, will, if all the above rules are attended to, be invariably dry, and free from white ants, which latter are the great dread of the living and the dead.

These are but general principles, the application of which we shall presently observe in detail, when we have to treat of the compass as indicating the numerical proportions of the breath and of the forms of nature.

I now proceed to consider the second division of the system of Feng-shui, called Su, or the numerical proportions of nature. Observing the heavens, the constant change of day and night, the numbers and distribution of the heavenly bodies, moving on, hosts of them, each in swift course, and yet never interfering with each other—I say observing this varied and yet harmonious whole, it struck the Chinese observer, that there are, at the basis of this grand scheme of heaven, mathematical principles; that all the heavenly bodies exist and move in certain numerical proportions. Again, observing our earth, with its constant revolutions of summer and winter, spring and autumn, growth and decay, life and death, the Chinese noticed, that here again the same mathematical order is repeated, that earth is but the reflex of heaven, the coarse material embodiment of the ideal mathematical problems, ethereally sketched on the firmament of heaven.

Now, to illustrate and fathom this scheme of numerical proportions, which connects and holds together heaven and earth, the ancient sages of China invented certain diagrams. I do not attribute any credence to the story of Foo-he

Rock-cut tombs and temples in mountains near Amoy.

observing a dragon-horse coming out of the river, bearing on its back the geometrical delineations of the great scheme of heaven and earth, in diagrfas and circles formed by the curling of the hairs. But the fact seems incontestable, that in the remotest times of Chinese antiquity certain diagrams were used to illustrate the numerical proportions of the universe. No matter who it was that first invented the scheme of diagrams, no matter whether he eliminated it from his own brain or by cogitating over the confused lines on the back of a tortoise, the fact remains that, more than 2,000 years ago, the Chinese had and used a scheme of diagrams essentially the same as that which is to the present day used by the ignorant and superstitious as a charm of ineffable efficacy, and frequently suspended over house-doors. However this set of eight diagrams may have originally been constructed, whether synthetically or analytically, the way in which its origin was afterwards explained is this.

Representing the superior creative male principle by one line, and the corresponding female principle by a line broken in two, then multiplying and combining them, four diagrams are obtained, viz:

1. $=$ two parallel lines, representing the great male principle.

2. $= =$ two parallel lines, each broken in two, representing the great female principle.

3. $==$ a line broken in two, with one parallel line below, called the little male.

4. $\overline{=}$ one unbroken line, with a parallel line, broken in two, below, called the little female.

The great male diagram was then taken as a symbol for the sun, the heat, the intellect, the eyes, etc. The great female diagram was considered to represent the planets, the night, the body, the mouth, etc.; whilst the little male diagram signified the moon, the cold, the passions, the ears, etc.; and the little female diagram stood for the stars, the daylight, the form, the nose, etc.

Proceeding then to combine these four diagrams with each other, in all possible forms, another set of eight diagrams was obtained. It is geometrically composed of the preceding four diagrams, but its primitive explanation was, I presume, based on a now antiquated view of the elements composing nature. I have already noticed more than once the enumeration of five elements, metal, wood, water, fire, and earth, now current in China. In the time when this set of eight diagrams was invented, quite a different enumeration of elements appears to have been in vogue. The Chinese must have then counted six elements, and named them as follows: thunder, wind, fire, ocean, water, and mountains. At any rate, one of the oldest classics of the Chinese, the Yih-king, explains this set of diagrams as follows: (1) three whole lines, representing the great male principle stand for heaven and designate the South; (2) three broken parallel lines representing the great female principle stand for earth and point to the North. Next follow what I take to signify the six elements of nature: (1) in the East, two whole lines with a broken line between, signify fire, for, says the Yih-king, in drying up the myriad of things there is nothing more parching than fire; (2) in the West, two broken lines with a whole line between, represent water, for in moistening the myriad of things there is nothing more humid than water; (3) in the South-West, two whole lines with one broken line on the inner side represent the wind, for in twirling round the myriad of things there is nothing more effective than wind; (4) in the North-East, two broken lines with one whole line on the inner side, correspond to thunder, for in agitating the myriad of things there is nothing more rapid than thunder; (5) in the South-East, two whole lines with one broken line on the outer side, represent vapour or the ocean, for in satisfying the myriad of things there is nothing more gratifying than the ocean; (6) in the North-West, two broken lines with one whole line on the outer side, signify mountains, for in bringing to a conclusion and gain commencing the myriad of things, there is nothing more perfect than the mountains. Thus, the Yih-king adds, water and fire overtaking and blending with each other, thunder and wind not opposing one another, and the mountains and oceans being pervaded by the same breath, nature can perform her transformations and complete and perfect the myriad of things.

To allow fancy and imaginative ingenuity still wider play, these eight diagrams are not only, as we have shown, made to correspond to the eight points of the compass, but also to eight different seasons. Even a set of eight different animals are made to answer to these eight diagrams, the first of which is said to represent the strength of a horse, the second the docility of an ox, the third is said to be pleasant like a pheasant, the fourth degrading like a swine, the fifth penetrating like a fowl, the sixth influential like a dragon, the seventh pleasing like a lamb, the eighth faithful like a dog.

To illustrate all the innumerable changes and permutations of nature, these eight diagrams were again multiplied with each other, and put through all possible combinations and thus another set of sixty-four diagrams was obtained, each having likewise a special name, special meaning and special occult virtues attached. This developement of the original system ascribed to Foo-he is however based on a different arrangement of the eight principle diagrams. The diagram for heaven which Foo-he's sytem placed in the South is now consigned to the North-West whilst the fire diagram, which the more ancient system placed in the East, now occupied the South. In like manner the earth diagram, formerly ruling the North, is now relegated to the South-West and its place assigned to the water diagram which formerly reigned in the West. Accordingly we have, in this new arrangement of the eight diagrams of Foo-he, the diagram for water in the North, that for thunder in the East, that for fire in the South, that for ocean in the West. The North-East is occupied by the diagram answering for mountains, the South-East by the wind diagram, whilst the diagram for earth is placed in the South-West, and that for heaven in the North West. This new arrangement of the original eight diagrams, and most especially its development into a set of sixty-four separate diagrams, is said to have been originated by Wen-wang, the reputed founder of the Chow dynasty, who, whilst undergoing a term of solitary confinement, amused himself by arranging and rearranging stems of straw on the basis of those eight diagrams, so that the various combinations of long and short stems of straw should represent the whole scheme of heaven and earth as pervaded by the male and female principles. We can readily believe that the Chinese, casting about for the inventor of this fanciful theory, hit upon the idea, that none but a man shut out from the world, none but a man whose brain is diseased by solitary confinement, could work out a system so ingenious indeed and marvellously fanciful, but so utterly devoid of all practical observation of nature.

This absence of direct connection with and practical application of the facts ascertained by observation of nature was of course more and more felt, the more the Chinese progressed in their knowledge of astronomy and in the other branches of natural science. That ancient system of diagrams, based on an antiquated theory of six terrestrial elements, makes no allowance for the influence of the five planets, which were in after ages supposed to exercise an almost paramount influence upon the destinies of the human race. The five planets seem to have been unknown even in the days of Confucius, at any rate they are never mentioned in the Chinese classics. Consequently the philosophers of the Sung dynasty finding the old system to clash with their popular views of astronomy, but having too much reverence for the sacred rust of antiquity to discard it altogether, retained the old diagrams, but worked them into a system, based on the idea, that the five planets (Venus, Jupiter, Mercury, Mars, and Saturn) and five corresponding terrestrial elements (metal, wood, water, fire and earth) contain as it were the principle solution of the great mystery of life. They ascribed to the five planets a central position, and searching out on this basis the numerical proportions of the universe, they arrived at the conclusion, that all heavenly bodies and all the powers and influences of heaven are arranged according to the decimal system. Applying, then, the ancient six elements which enter into the plan of the four and eight diagrams, and which indeed refer exclusively to earth and not to heaven— applying, I say, these ancient sets of four diagrams and of eight diagrams to terrestrial relations alone, they came to the conclusion that all the formations of earth, all terrestrial relations, are based on the duodecimal system. Thus they invented a set of ten symbolic characters or numbers intended to explain the mysteries of heaven, and called them the ten heavenly stems. Then they drew up another series of twelve symbolic characters or numbers and used them as the mathematical key to solve all the problems relating to the earth, calling them the twelve terrestrial branches. They, moreover, distinguished in both the ten heavenly stems and the twelve terrestrial branches, the even and uneven numbers. All the uneven numbers they declared, in obedience to the rules laid down in the Yih-king, to refer to the male principle, all the even numbers to the female principle in nature. Again, they divided, likewise adopting a rule of the ancient system, the ten heavenly stems into five couples, but made each couple correspond not only to one of the five elements, but also to one of the five planets. The twelve terrestrial branches were made to signify the above-mentioned twelve signs of the zodiac, also the twelve points of the Chinese compass and the twelve divisions of the day (each division comprising two hours). Again, by combining the two series and joining the first of the twelve terrestrial branches to the first of the ten heavenly stems, then joining the second characters of each series and going on through the ten stems six times and through the twelve branches five times, they obtained a set of sixty cyclic characters, which they used to designate successive days and years, and which multiplied by six gave the three hundred and sixty degrees of the ecliptic.

Here we have then a series of logarithmic formulæ, skilfully designed, to compromise all the numerical proportions which the Chinese ascribe to the universe and intricate enough to perplex any ordinary mind, and to awe by its mysteriousness the ignorant mass of the people. Skilful and ingenious manipulation of such a system naturally enables a man to impose upon the superstitious multitude, and consequently we find, that all the different arts of divination in China—astrology, geomancy, horoscopy, phrenology, chiromancy and so on—are all based upon this system of numbers. For geomantic purposes, with which alone we have to do here, all the above-mentioned diagrams and series of computations have been combined for practical and handy use in the shape of a compass, with a magnetic needle in the centre, and all the different diagrams and cyclic characters with all the elements that enter into calculation inscribed in concentric circles on the board surrounding the needle.

The use of the magnetic needle suggested to me the possibility that the Chinese might possibly have some empirical knowledge of terrestrial magnetism, and use the magnetic needle to observe the declination, inclination and intensity of the magnetic currents which run through the crust of the earth and which are nowadays being carefully watched by modern meteorologists in America and Europe. But I am sorry to say I have not been able to find even the slightest empirical knowledge of the fact, that a freely suspended magnet indicates by its movements the inclination, declination and intensity of the magnetic currents in the earth.

To begin with the outmost of the circles inscribed on the compass plate, we find this circle (XVIII) divided into twenty-eight portions of unequal size, on each of which there is the name of one of the twenty-eight constellations through which the moon passes in her course along the ecliptic, with the number of degress each constellation occupies. This circle therefore represent the moon's orbit and its use is to determine not only the lunar influences generally, but also the influence which each particular constellation is supposed to exercise on any given spot. Every Chinese calendar gives a series of twenty-eight tables containing a minute enumeration of the geomantic affinities ascribed to each constellation, but it will suffice here to state that fifteen of them are put down in the calendar as unlucky, thirteen as lucky. To enable the geomancer, however, to determine the lucky or unlucky lunar influences of any locality with perfect accuracy, the next circle (XVII) represents again the ecliptic, but divided into three hundred and sixty degress, of which some are marked as lucky; whilst on the next circle (XVI) the successive odd numbers of three hundred and sixty-six degrees are marked, in twenty-eight portions corresponding to the twenty-eight constellations of the XVII circle, thus enabling the geomancer to pronounce with regard to every inch of ground and with reference to every day in the year whether the female or male principle prevails here, for the odd numbers represent the male, the even numbers (left blank) the female principle.

Proceeding farther towards the centre the next circle (XV), divided into sixty portions, is intended to illustrate the influence of the five planets in their relation to the five elements: metal, wood, water, fire, earth. These five terms are seriatim inscribed on the circle in different combinations, now destroying each other, then again indifferent to each other, then again producing each other, and so on. Each element occurs twelve times, but the element wood is in one place interpolated, where it is placed with the element fire to the right and left, occupying two degrees which correspond to the tenth and eleventh degree of the constellation "bushel" (six stars in the shoulder and bow of Sagittarius). The geomancer referring to any particular locality is thus enabled to say not only by which particular planets the spot is influenced, but also whether the terrestrial element prevailing there is in harmony with elements ruling the adjoining places to the right and left. Suppose, for instance, a certain spot is indicated by the compass as being under the influence of Mars. Well, the corresponding terrestrial element is fire. Now, if the compass there indicates wood to the left and water to the right, the omen is very bad, because water destroys fire and fire destroys wood. But suppose the compass indicated the element earth to the left of the element fire, and to its right the element wood, this would be a favourable conjunction, because wood produces fire and fire produces earth. The elements are however in places so arranged that they are seriatim indifferent to each other, neither producing nor destroying each other, which of course is likewise considered a favourable conjunction.

The next circle (XIV) is formed by two concentric lines of characters divided into sixty portions. The inner line of characters gives thirteen different combinations of the ten heavenly stems, so arranged, that each character signifies at the same time a certain element and either an even (female) or uneven (male) number. Each of these thirteen combinations of elements (or planets) begins with the element (or planet) wood (i.e. Jupiter), and alternately, now with the number one (male) and then with the number two (female). The twelfth combination only, beginning with the element (planet) fire (i.e. Mars) and the number three (male) makes an exception. Out of the thirteen combinations eight contain the complete series of elements (or planets) in the order in which they produce each other (wood, fire, earth, metal, water). The remaining five combinations contain four elements (or planets) each. Three of these combinations give the elements in couples, in accordance with the order of production. Two combinations only give the elements (or planets) in couples, the elements (or planets) of which produce each other in the one and destroy each other in the other couple. The corresponding outer line of characters, divided into twelve spaces, subjoins to every five characters of the inner line one of the twelve zodiacal signs five times repeated. Consequently each of the twelve divisions of this circle contains on the outer line one zodiacal sign placed in conjunction with five different elements (or planets) on the inner line, but in every zodiacal sign the arrangement and mutual relation of the elements (or planets) is different.

Proceeding farther towards the centre the next circle (XIII) in sixty divisions gives forty-eight characters, referring each to a different symbol of those famous sixty-four diagrams of Wen-wang which I have mentioned above. But of these forty-eight different diagrams there are six, which go to form the set of eight diagrams, viz., earth, ocean, fire, thunder, wind, and mountains, and which are here given twice, in different locations; six others, not belonging to the set of eight diagrams, are each given twice side by side. For the explanation of these forty-eight diagrams the geomancer resorts to the table given in every calendar, where each of these diagrams is given and the lucky and unlucky days (for geomantic work) pointed out.

The next circle (XII) is divided into twenty-four divisions, each of which is subdivided into five compartments. The second and fourth compartments in each of the twenty-four divisions have a double row of characters inscribed all round. The inner line of characters gives alternately through each division, now the two symbols for fire (ping-ting)—which signify also the numbers three (male) and four (female)—and then the two symbols for metal (kang-sin)—or the numbers seven (male) and eight (female)—repeated twice in each division; the series being ping-ting ping-ting, kang-sin kang-sin. In the corresponding outer line the twelve terrestrial branches or signs of the zodiac are given below the above-mentioned symbols in twelve divisions, each division having one zodiacal sign four times repeated in identical characters. The use of this circle therefore is to connect in rotation ·each of the twelve signs of the zodiac with either of the two elements fire or metal, or with the planets Mars or Venus, as also with certain male or female members.

The following circle (XI) is identical with another counting VIII from the centre, only the characters inscribed on them are so arranged that, for instance, the symbol designating due North is on the one circle to the left, on the other to the right of the line which runs due North between them. Now, on both these circles, divided in twenty-four divisions, are inscribed seriatim one or other of the twelve branches, alternating with one or other of the ten stems (but omitting the two stems which designate earth), whilst after every five of these characters one of the following four diagrams (taken from the set of eight diagrams) is inserted: the diagrams for heaven, earth, mountains, and wind. This circle therefore combines the twelve points of the Chinese compass, with simultaneous reference to the elements—wood, fire, metal, and water, to the planets—Jupiter, Mars, Venus, and Mercury, and to the four geomantic principles—heaven, earth, mountains, and wind.

The next circle (X) gives the minor divisions of the compass. It is divided into sixty spaces, on which however not only the bearings of the compass are inscribed, but also the bearings of the afore-mentioned ten heavenly stems and four geomantic principles. It reads, for instance, from East to South as follows: Due. East. 7 (metal), 3 (fire). 3 (fire), 7 (metal). Due two (wood). 5 (earth), 5 (earth). Due E.S.E. 3/4 E. 7 (metal), 3 (fire). 3 (fire), 7 (metal). Due Wind. 5 (earth), 5 (earth). Due S.S.E. 3/4 E. 7 (metal), 3 (fire). 3 (fire), 7 (metal). Due Fire. 5 (earth), 5 (earth). Due South. The numbers 7, 3, 5 mean of course fractions of ten, or subdivisions of the compass. The words 7 (metal) 3 (fire), for instance, mean that seven-tenths of this subdivision of the compass are ruled by the element metal, and three-tenths of the same space by the element fire.

With this circle corresponds the next (IX) which gives like-wise in sixty divisions two concentric rows of characters. This circle with its characters is identically the same with the above-described XIV circle and with another counting V from the centre. Only the inscriptions on the three circles are in different positions, so that, for instance, the first character of the XIV circle (inner row) is nearly East, that of the V circle nearly E.S.E., whilst the first of the IX circle is between them.

The next (VIII) circle is identically the same in all but position of characters with the XI, and supplements that circle by making the line in which the influence of each symbol runs more prominent.

The following circle (VII) is divided like the VIII and XI into twenty-four divisions, each division representing one of the twenty-four solar terms or twenty-four periods corres-ponding to the day on which the sun enters the first and fifteenth degree of one of the zodiacal signs. This circle is therefore a miniature calendar, and its use is to determine the season during which a house may be erected or a tomb built in any given place. These twenty-four seasons being however not only under the influence of the sun, but also under that of the five elements and the five planets, the next two circles exhibit the influence which these elements and planets exercise on each of the twenty-four seasons of the year.

The first of them (VI) brings to bear upon each season one of the twelve zodiacal signs and two planets or elements, fire (Mars) and metal (Venus). The second (V), however, brings not only two but all the five elements and planets, in addition to the twelve signs of the zodiac, to bear upon the twenty-four seasons. This circle is divided into twelve distinct portions, with a blank space between each, and each division contains on the outer row of characters one zodiacal sign five times repeated, whilst on the corresponding portion of the inner row five different celestial stems are inscribed. But these stems are arranged in twelve different combinations, giving alternately, now in even now in uneven numbers, the various elements or planets.

The succeeding circle (IV) is divided into twenty-four equal parts, on which are inscribed—(1) the twelve zodiacal signs, the uneven numbers being marked red as peculiarly auspicious, viz. Aries, Gemini (who represent the white tiger), Leo (who represents the azure dragon), Libra, Sagittarius, and Aquarius; (2) eight of the ten celestial stems, viz. two characters for the element water, two for wood, two for fire, and two for metal; (3) four symbols belonging to the eight diagrams, viz. heaven (marked red), earth (marked red), wind, and water. This circle is essentially the same as VIII and XI, and their identity is made still more prominent by the equality of breadth of space and size of characters. The only difference in these three circles is that the characters are placed in different position, indicating more prominently the exact line in which the influence of each symbol proceeds.

The next circle (III) joins to the twelve zodiacal signs those nine stars of the northern bushel which we mentioned above. They are arranged here in twenty-four compartments, one, called the breaker of the phalanx, occurring three times; three others, called the military star, the literary star, and the star of purity, each four times; three others, called the avaricious wolf, official emoluments, and the wide door, occur each twice; and the remaining two, the left-hand assistant, and the right-hand assistant, each once.

The following circle (II) gives, in twenty-four divisions, of which however every alternate one is left blank, (I) the diagrams for heaven, earth, mountains, and wind, (2) eight heavenly stems in couples, of which each character refers to a different number, element or planet. The sequence is as follows: (1) wind, (2) number two wood and number three fire, (3) wind, (4) earth, (5) number four fire and number

seven metal, (6) earth, (7) heaven, (8) number eight metal
and number nine water, (9) heaven, (10) mountains, (11)
number ten water and number one wood, (12) mountains.
It will be noticed that the four couples of elements (planets)
here mentioned are so arranged, that each couple contains an
even (female) and uneven (male) number, and that the
elements (planets) they refer to are in accordance with the
order of production.

The first and inmost circle gives in eight compartments the
names of eight zodiacal signs; Leo, Gemini, Sagittarius,
Capricorn, Pisces, Cancer, Virgo, and Libra.

Now, of course, when the compass is consulted with
reference to any given spot, it is not only one of these
eighteen circles, but every one of them, that is made to contribute some quota towards the determination of the lucky
or unlucky aspects of the place in question. The result, therefore, is that for every single spot quite a number of bewilder-
ing conjunctions can be enumerated, which produce with the
uninitiated the belief, that this compass is almost mysterious
compound of supernatural wisdom. And I think we must
acknowledge that it is indeed a clever contrivance, making
the most of a very rudimentary knowledge of astronomy, for
it comprises in one perspicuous arrangement, all the different
principles of Chinese physical science, the male and female
principles, the eight diagrams, the sixty-four diagrams, the
solar orbit, the lunar ecliptic, the three hundred and sixty
degrees of longitude, the days of the year, and five planets,
the five elements, the twenty-eight constellations, the twelve
zodiacal signs, the nine stars of the bushel, the twenty-four
seasons, and the twelve points of the compass.

The uncommon people know all these terms by name, but
not understanding their meaning, they regard the terms themselves with a certain reverential awe, supposing them to
exercise some mysterious magic influence. Now, the
geomancer, taking advantage of this popular prejudice, comes
to them with this compass in his hands, of which the

ordinary Chinaman understands next to nothing and pro-
nouncing his judgment with reference to any given spot in a
mystifying learned jargon, his apocalyptic utterances are
received with superstitious dread even where there is not
much faith in the system. The geomancer himself knows very
well that his predictions are all guesswork, based on what
experience he manages to collect in the course of his practice.
But he also knows that his prophesies are sometimes realised
in consequence of the very fear they inspire, and though his
predictions may more frequently be disproved by actual
events, yet he comforts himself by thinking, that his compass
after all makes money flow if not into the lap of his
employers yet certainly into his own pocket.

We now come to the third division of the system of Feng-shui, the doctrine of nature's breath. Nature, as I have had occasion to remark before, is looked upon by the Chinese observer as a living breathing organism, and we cannot be surprised, therefore, to find the Chinese gravely discussing the inhaling and exhaling breath of nature. In fact, with the distinction of these two breaths, the expanding breath, as they call it, and reverting breath, they explain almost every phenomenon in nature. Between heaven and earth there is nothing so important, so almighty and omnipresent as this breath of nature. It enters into every stem and fibre, and through it heaven and earth and every creature live and move and have their being. Nature's breath is, in fact, but the spiritual energy of the male and female principles. Thus at the commencement the congelation of the transforming breath of nature is the change from nothing into being of the male principle the exhaustion of the transforming breath of nature is the change from existence to non-existence of the female principle of nature. When therefore in the beginning these two principles first issued from "the great absolute", it was then that nature's breath first went forth.

A philosopher's retreat in the Foochung Hill, province of Che-keang. Rock-cut steps give access to the fishing pools.

But at first nature's breathing was confused and chaotic, so that for some time heaven and earth were not divided, but when nature's breath reverted, and exhalation and inhalation regularly succeeded each other, heaven and earth, the male and female principles, were divided and everything in nature was produced in its proper order. Even now, whenever the breath of nature first advances or expands, something like an unshapen fœtus is created, which constitutes the germlike beginning of future developments. This shapeless incipient origin of things being light and pure, but not yet possessing any determinate form, belongs to the male, and may be called the superior principles of nature; but when the determinate shape has been assumed, it manifestly presents itself to view, and constitutes the exact form of things, possessing body, colour, shape and manner. This, being heavy, gross and cognizable to human sense, belong to the female, and may be called the inferior principle, or in other words, one advancing and one reverting breath, regularly succeeding each other, are the condition of the constant sucession of growth and decay, of life and death in the physical world.

The two breaths of nature are, however, essentially but one breath. The male and female principles, uniting, constitute the beginning of things; when they disperse they cause decay, dissolution and death. Sometimes they disperse and again unite. Thus, after their termination they again commence, which constitutes the principle of reproduction, going on throughout nature without intermission. As to the breath that pervades human beings, the energies of nature must here also sometimes get exhausted, and death is that which no man can avoid. At death, the grosser parts of man's animal soul descend and return to earth, but the finer parts of spiritual nature diffuse and expand throughout the world and become either a cloud or a light that appears occasionally, will-o'-the-wisps, or *ignes fatui*, or such like, or a fragrant vapour that sometimes nobody knows how, affects men's senses and causes them to feel dull, sad and depressed.

Now, this breath of nature, with its constant pulsations, with its ceaseless permutations of expansion and contraction, shows itself in the varied conditions of the atmosphere in a six-fold form, being the originating cause of cold, heat, dryness, moisture, wind and fire. These are sometimes called the six breaths of nature. These six breaths then produce, under the combined influence of the five planets and the five elements, the twenty-four seasons, which are therefore generally called the twenty-four breaths of nature. The breath of nature allied to the element wood, and guided by Jupiter, produces rain; combined with the element metal and ruled by Venus, the breath of nature produce fine weather; joining the element fire and influenced by Mars, the breath of nature produces heat; supported by the element water and ruled by Mercury, the breath of nature produces cold; and with the help of the element earth and influenced by Saturn, it causes wind. This is the whole system of Chinese meteorology.

But the question now arises, how can we, quite apart from the general working of nature's breath, determine, with reference to any given locality, whether there is a favourable or unfavourable breath there, or any breath at all?

Here, again, the Feng-shui system makes use of the allegory of the azure dragon and the white tiger. We have remarked above that the surface of the earth is but the dim mirror of the configurations, powers and influences of the heavens, that therefore every constellation of heaven has its counterpart on earth. We have also noticed (p.14) that one of the four quadrants of the starry heavens, the one in the East or to the left of the looker-on, is ruled by a spirit called the azure dragon, embodying as it were the combined influences of seven constellations. The western or right-hand quadrant, comprising also seven constellations, is represented by a spirit called the white tiger. The azure dragon and the white tiger are therefore but emblems indicating the subtle influences, the vital breath of the eastern (male) and western (female) divisions of the firmament. Wherever there is nature's breath pulsating, there will be visible on earth some elevation of the ground. Where nature's breath is running through the crust of the earth, the veins and arteries, so to speak, will be traceable. But nature's breath contains a two-fold element, a male and female, positive and negative, expanding and reverting breath, resembling, as we in modern English would put it, two magentic currents, or, as the Chinese put it, the azure dragon and the white tiger. Where there is a true dragon, there will be also a tiger, and the two will be traceable in the outlines of mountains or hills running in a tortuous and curved course. Moreover, there will be discernible the dragon's trunk and limbs, nay, even the very veins and arteries of his body, running off from the dragon's heart in the form of ridges or chains of hills. As a rule, therefore, there will be an accumulation of vital breath near the dragon's waist, whilst near the extremities of his body the energy of nature's breath is likely to be exhausted. At a distance of twenty li, or six miles, it is said the breath becomes feeble and ineffective. But even near the dragon's heart, the breath of nature, unless well kept together by surrounding hills and mountains, will be scattered. Where the frontage of any given spot, though enjoying an abundance of vital breath, is broad and open on all sides, admitting the wind from all the four quarters, there the breath will be of no advantage, for the wind scatters it before it can do any good. Again, suppose there is a piece of ground with plenty of vital breath, and flanked by hills, which tend to retain the breath, yet the water courses near the place run off in straight and rapid course, there also the breath is scattered and wasted before it can serve any beneficial purposes. Only in places where the breath of nature is well kept together, being shut in to the right and left and having a drainage carrying off the water in a winding tortuous course, there are the best indications of a permanent supply of vital breath being found there. Building a tomb or a house in such a place will ensure prosperity, wealth and honour.

As a general rule it is observed, that whenever one meets with doubtful ground which shows no clear indications of the dragon's veins, it is best to look for the most secluded retired corner, for in retirement it is that tiger and dragon are most closely intertwined, and there the breath is gathered most abundantly. And suppose ground has been found where both dragon and tiger are completely delineated, the rule is then to look near the junction of dragon and tiger for some little hollow or little mound, or in short some sudden transition from male to female or from female to male ground. For the body of the dragon and the surrounding hills should always exhibit both male and female characteristics up to the very point where the luck-bringing site is to be chosen.

I have hitherto only spoken of the natural and beneficial breath of nature. But there is also a poisonous deadly exhalation of nature's breath, and it is one of the supposed advantages of the Feng-shui system that it points out and warns people against a place where the erection of a tomb or house would entail loss of life and calamities over coming generations. Very frequently, it is said, there are places showing all the outward appearances of good dragon ground, and betraying no visible sign of the existence of malign influences, and yet the ground would bring untold calamities and utter desolation on any family that would venture to choose a site there for a tomb or a dwelling place. In such cases it is only the compass that will indicate the presence of a noxious breath, by marking the disharmony of the planetary influences and the discord of the elements.

But in general the existence of a pernicious breath will betray itself by outward indications. Wherever there is a hill or mountain, abruptly rising up from the ground, and running up in bold straight lines, or shows an exceedingly rugged rough appearance, without any gradual slopings, there is dangerous breath there. Generally speaking, all straight

lines are evil indications, but most especially when a straight
line points towards the spot where a site has been chosen.
Even suppose you have found a place where both the dragon
to the left and the tiger to the right are curved each like a
bow, but from the side of each, ridges are running down in
straight lines, resembling each an arrow laid on a bow—that
would be an absolutely dangerous configuration. Or, suppose
you have found a place abounding in good auspices, but some
distance opposite you there is a straight running ridge or
water shed, or say a railway embankment, by no means
pointing in the direction of your site, but running across your
frontage in a straight line—there would be caused by this line
a deadly breath, ruining all your fortunes and those of your
descendants.

As straight lines of ridges or chains of hills are supposed
to produce malign influences, thus it is also with creeks,
canals or rivers, that run off in straight lines. Water is in the
Feng-shui system always looked upon as the emblem of
wealth and affluence. Where the water runs off in a straight
course, it will cause the property of people dwelling there to
run off and dissipate like water. Tortuous, crooked lines
are the indications of a beneficial breath, and will serve to
retain the vital breath where it exists.

Another indication of the existence of a malign breath
are detached rocks and boulders, unless they are screened
and covered by trees and bushes. There are many instances
given in geomantic books of tombs situated near rocks and
loose boulders, but the latter being screened by dense
vegetation and shaded by high trees, the tomb in question
exercised for generations the most beneficial influence,
heaping rank, honour, wealth, longevity, progeny and so
forth upon the families whose ancestors were buried there.
But by and by, unbelief in Feng-shui, or avidity, or the
hatred of a malicious enemy caused the trees to be felled and
the shrubs which screened the boulders to be cut down,
whereupon immediately sudden disgrace and misfortunes

came upon those families; they were deprived of their rank, of their emoluments, their wealth scattered, and their descendants had to go out upon the highways of life to beg and starve.

Hongkong, with its abundance of rocks and boulders scattered about on the hillside, abounds accordingly in malign breath, and the Chinese think our Government very wise in eandeavouring to plant trees everywhere on the hill to screen these harbingers of evil. But the most malicious influence under which Hongkong suffers is caused by that curious rock on the edge of the hill near Wanchai. It is distinctly seen from Queen's Road East, and foreigners generally see in it Cain and Abel, Cain slaying his brother. The Chinese take the rock to represent a female figure which they call the bad woman, and they firmly and seriously believe that all the immorality of Hong-kong, all the recklessness and vice of Taip'ingshan are caused by that wicked rock. So firm in this belief impressed upon the lowest classes of Hongkong that those who profit from immoral practices actually go and worship that rock, spreading out offerings and burning frankincense at its foot. None dares to injure it, and I have been told by many otherwise sensible people that several stonecutters who attempted to quarry at the base of that rock died a sudden death immediately after the attempt.

Now, all these evil influences, whether they be caused by straight lines of hills or water courses of by rocks and boulders, can be fended off or counteracted. The best means to keep off and absorb such noxious exhalations is to plant trees at the back of your abode and keep a tank or pond with a constant supply of fresh water in front of your house. This is the reason why in South China every village, every hamlet, every isolated house has a little grove of bamboos or trees behind and a pond in front. A pagoda, however, or a wooded hill, answers the same purpose, and for this reason the Heights of Canton, with their five-storied pagoda, are supposed to fend off the evil breath of nature and to protect the whole city. Another device to keep off malign influences is to place opposite your house gate a shield or octagonal board with the emblems of the male and female principles, or the eight diagrams painted thereon, and to give the pathway leading up to your front door a curved or tortuous direction. Lions carved in stone or dragons of burnt clay also answer the same purpose, and may be placed either in front of a building or on the top of the roof; but by far the best and effective means is to engage a geomancer, to do what he says, and to pay him well.

A geomancer's compass.

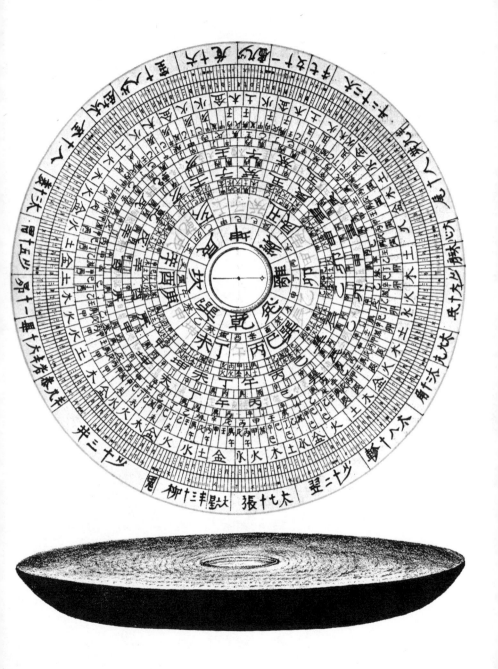

5 • NATURE'S FORMS OF APPEARANCE

We now come to the last division of the system of Feng-shui—the doctrine of nature's outlines and forms of appearance. This section, however, forms merely a practical application of the general rules and ideas laid down in the proceding chapters, and I need not therefore enter upon details at great length. I have already spoken of those elevations of the ground which indicate the presence of nature's breath, with its two currents of male and female, positive and negative energy, symbolically called dragon and tiger. The relative position and configuration of these two, the dragon and tiger, as indicated by hills or mountains, is the most important point, as regards the outlines and forms of the earth's surface. I will not enter into an enumeration of all those configurations which make the relative position, extent and direction of these two symbolic elements favourable or unfavourable. Suffice it to say that they are most happily placed when they form a complete horse-shoe, that is to say where two ridges of hills starting from one point run out to the right and left in a graceful curve their extremities gently turning inwards each other. Such a formation of hills or mountains is the sure index of the presence of a true

In the district of the Two Peaks, Chen-si province. These mountains are rich in gold and other minerals, but the feng-shui of the area was considered even more precious and mining was forbidden. Tartar guards were stationed here to deter prospectors.

dragon and—if other conjunctions counteract it not—the influence of a locality, chosen at the point where dragon and tiger start to the right and left, will be all that can be desired.

Another important element in the doctrine of the outward forms of nature is the direction of the watercourses. We have had occasion to allude to this more than once, and the chief point is, that water running off in straight lines or forming in its course sharp angles is absolutely dangerous. A curved and tortuous course is the best augury of the existence of beneficial influences. But the junction of two watercourses is likewise an element that should not be overlooked. The junction should take place in a graceful curve, and the con-joined waters roll on in tortuous course crossing and recross-ing the plain.

A third subject that calls for attention here is the form and shape of the hills, especially the outlines of their summit. I have remarked above that the summits of hills and mountains are the embodiment of certain heavenly bodies. It is there-fore one of the first requirements of a geomancer that he should be able to tell at a moment's glance which star is represented by any given mountain. As to the planets and their counterparts on earth, the rules by which each mountain may be referred to the one or other of the five planets are very simply. If a peak rises up bold and straight, running out into a sharp point, it is identified with Mars and declared to represent the element fire. If the point of a similarly shaped mountain is broken off and flat but comparatively narrow, it is said to be the embodiment of Jupiter and to represent the element wood. If the top of a mountain forms an extensive plateau, it is the representative of Saturn, and the element earth dwells there. If a mountain runs up high but its peak is softly rounded, it is called Venus and represents the element metal. A mountain whose top has the shape of a cupola is looked upon as the representative of Mercury, and the element water rules there.

Now of course, where there are several mountains or hills

in close proximity, it is all-important to find out whether the planets and the elements, which these mountains individually represent, form a harmonious peaceful union, for the luck of a place depends in a great measure upon this, that the planets and elements influencing it should be friendly or allied to each other, either producing each other or indifferent to each other. Suppose there is close to a hill resembling Jupiter and therefore representing the element wood, another with the outlines of Mars and corresponding to the element fire, it is manifest that this is a most dangerous conjunction. For instance, the peak of Hongkong, presenting the outlines of Jupiter, is under the influence of wood. Now, at the foot of the peak there is the hill called Taip'ingshan, with the outlines of Mars, and therefore the representative of fire. Now, a pile of wood with fire at the bottom—what is the consequence? Why, it is no wonder that most fires in Hongkong occur in the Taip'ingshan district. We see, therefore, it is most important to consider not only to which planet each hill or mountain belongs, but also the mutual relation, friendly or destructive, of the several planets and elements represented by the different peaks.

More obscure is the method by which the presence of so-called nine stars of the northern bushel is detected. These nine stars, with their fanciful names and dreadful influences, have no fixed outlines to indicate their characteristics and facilitate their indentification, but are to be chiefly recognized by the indication of the compass.

In general the association of ideas connected with the outlines of hills and mountains is of great importance. For instance, if a hill resembles in its general contour the form of a broad couch, then its influence will make your sons and grandsons die a premature and violent death. If you build on a mountain which resembles a boat turned bottom upwards, your daughters will always be ill, and your sons spend their days in prison. If a mountain reminds one in its general outlines of a bell, whilst at the top there are the outlines of

Venus, such a mountain will cause the seven stars of the Great Bear to throw a deadly light upon you which will render you and all the members of your family childless. Most dangerous are also hills that resemble the one or other of the following objects: a basket, a ploughshare, the eye of a horse, a turtle, a terrace, a meadow.

There are many more rules referring to the forms and outlines of the earth's surface. But I think the above will suffice to give my readers a tolerably clear idea of the practical teachings of the Feng-shui system.

There is only one point left to be adverted to, and this is the art of improving the natural configuration of any given place. Heaven, it is said, requires the aid of man to carry out its scheme of justice. Earth requires the aid of man to bring its products to absolute perfection. Neither heaven nor earth are complete in themselves, but leave the last finish of everything to man. Consequently, as regards the natural outlines of the earth's surface, there is much room left for the active interference of man. The influence of the planets and the five elements is very great, but it is not all. The influence of the natural configuration of the ground is very powerful in its influence upon the destiny of men, but man may alter the natural configurations, and improve the aspects of any unfavourable locality. If there is any elevation not high enough, he can make it higher; if any natural watershed is running in a straight line dangerous to life and property, he can either remove it or turn it into a favourable direction. If there is a mountain representing Mars and the element of fire why he has simply to cut off the point of the mountain and thus convert Mars into Jupiter. Or, if there is a mountain disturbing the harmony of the surroundings because it bears the outlines of Jupiter, why he has merely to round off the outlines of its peak and Jupiter is changed into Venus. This is frequently done, and especially travellers will have noticed a pointed mound here or there on the very top of a high but somewhat flat mountain. This mound is raised to convert that mountain, which being flat corresponds to Saturn, into Mars, for the element fire, though itself never giving good ground for a tomb or house, is absolutely required as an element to enter into the general configuration of the surroundings.

We see, therefore, it is left in a great measure to man's foresight and energy to turn his fortunes into any channel he pleases, to modify and regulate the influences which heaven and earth bring to bear upon him, and it is the boast of the Feng-shui system that it teaches man how to rule nature and his own destiny by showing him how heaven and earth rule him.

We have hitherto looked upon Feng-shui as derived chiefly from the teachings of Choo-he and other philosophers of the Sung dynasty. And certainly, when we regard Feng-shui as a recognized popular system of physical science, as a methodical combination of certain philosophical ideas for definite practical purposes, we can scarcely trace its origin beyond that period so justly called the Augustan age of Chinese literature. But the most prominent ideas and practices which go to make up this system of popular superstition can be followed up to very ancient times. The leading principles of Feng-shui have their roots in remote antiquity, and it would not be exaggeration to say, that, though indeed modern Feng-shui was not a distinct branch of study or a separate profession before the Sung dynasty (A.D. 960-1126), yet the history of the leading ideas and practices of Feng-shui is the history of Chinese philosophy.

The deepest root of the Feng-shui system grew out of that excessive and superstitious veneration of the spirits of ancestors, which, though philosophical minds like that of Confucious might construe it on an exclusively moral basis as simply an expression of filial piety, was with the mass of the

Altar-piece in the great temple at Ting-hai, Chusan, once the richest in China. The Queen of Heaven, standing on a dolphin within a grotto, corresponds to the Christian Virgin.

Chinese people the fruitful soil from which the poisonous weed of rank superstition sprang up in profusion. Ancestral worship naturally implied the idea that the spirits of deceased ancestors could and would somehow influence the fortunes of their descendants. This superstitious notion, the existence of which can be shewn in the most ancient records of Chinese thought that we possess, is the moving spring and leading instinct of the whole Feng-shui system.

The next step in the direction of Feng-shui, which the superstitious mind of antiquity took was to connect this supposed influence of deceased ancestors with the locality of their tombs and the topographical character of the surroundings of each grave. In the most primitive ages of Chinese antiquity no such custom can be shewn to have been in vogue. But we have some distinct traces of the first budding of this idea. In the times of the early dawn of Chinese history, which I place not earlier than the Chow dynasty (B.C. 1122), ordinary people, it is reported, used to be buried in the plain, princes on low hills, emperors under a mound on the top of high mountains. Here we have the first indication of a degree of importance being attached not only to the general situation of the tomb, but also to its construction, viz., the erection, in the case of imperial tombs, of a high mound, supposed, no doubt, to protect the back of the tomb; the dragon in fact, of future ages.

Again, it is reported, on the authority of Confucius, that in ancient times graves were so constructed that the head of the deceased should point towards the North. The words of the Li-ke, where the passage occurs, are "the dead have their heads placed towards the North, the living face the South"; and the Confucian commentator explains the reason of this mode of interment by saying, that the North was viewed as ruled by the female principle, the South by the male principle; that death and decomposition were considered to belong to the female or reverting breath of nature, life and vigour to the influence of the expanding or male energy. This indicates another step having been made in the direction of Feng-shui: the male and female energies of nature, and the compass distinctions of North and South, are brought to bear upon the position and construction of the tomb.

The mound over the grave, which originally was the prerogative of imperial tombs, was in course of time adopted by all classes of people. In the period immediately preceding the time of Confucius it appears that it was generally considered important to have a mound of earth on every tomb. The very attitude that Confucius, the admirer of primitive antiquity, assumed with reference to this custom, which he deemed an unwarrantable innovation, shews clearly that the ancient form of interment had been deviated form and that customs and ideas were in and before his time connected with the construction of tombs which he considered himself bound to protest against.

Taking all the above-mentioned indications into account, it would seem undeniable, that long before Confucius the attention of mourners was directed to the importance of carefully choosing the site for a tomb and constructing the tomb itself in a certain manner prescribed by custom. It is natural to suppose that this was done with a view to guard against calamities, or to ensure prosperity which might be caused, in the opinion of superstitious worshippers of ancestral spirits, by the spirit to whom the tomb in question was dedicated. In short, the elementary principles of Feng-shui appear to have been practised centuries before Confucius, unconsciously, as it were, by superstitious people. But there is nothing to prove that Feng-shui was reduced to a science, that it was practised methodically as a profession. As long as the ancient belief in a supreme personal God exercised any influence on the people, the afore-mentioned ideas floating about among those influenced by superstition could not form themselves into a system, which required the notion of materialistic fatalism for a centre round which they might gather to take the definite form and shape of a system like that of Feng-shui. Chinese devotees of Feng-shui try indeed to adduce proof that in those earliest times Feng-shui was a recognized branch of science. The passage they rely on is, however, too vague to warrant such a conclusion. Speaking of the diagrams of Foo-he, the Yih-king says, "the sage looks up to heaven and (with the help of the diagrams) he observes all the celestial phenomena, he contemplates the earth and (using the same diagrams) examines the outlines of the ground." But the very sentence that follows shows that this passage does not refer to anything like Feng-shui—"he traces up the origin of all things and follows again their existence to the end; thus he comprehends the theory of life and death." It is clear therefore that this passage simply refers to the use of the diagrams as applied to the universe in general. There is not the slightest evidence to show that the diagrams of Foo-he or Wen-wang were ever applied, in those early times, to the geomantic position of tombs and the determination of the influence which tombs were believed to exercise upon the fortunes of men.

The second period in the history of Feng-shui may be said to extend from Confucius (B.C. 550) to the rise of the Han dynasty (B.C. 202). It was in the power of Confucius and his disciples, Mencius and Sun-tze, who exercised a strong influence on the minds of their countrymen during this period, to repress and rectify the superstitious notions already floating about among the people and tending towards a regular system of geomancy, by assuming a definite attitude, denouncing superstition and substituting an enlightened theory on the subject. But he and his disciples, though personally free from superstition, contended themselves with urging a reform of morality according to the pattern of the ancient sages, without venturing to grapple with the superstitions that were gathering round the ancient form of ancestral worship. In one word, they remained neutral, and the consequence was that superstition spread farther and farther. The position which Confucius and his disciples took with regard to those early symptoms of geomantic superstition is characteristically illustrated by an anecdote the truth of which has never been impugned. Confucius, having with some difficulty discovered the grave of his father, had it opened and the remains of this mother buried together with those of his father. On this occasion it was suggested that, in accordance with the custom of the time, a mound should be raised over the grave. Confucius, though he remarked that this was not in accordance with the rules of the ancients, did not oppose it, but—it is said—soon after the mound had been raised, a sudden fall of rain washed it away and levelled the ground!

This little incident shows that he himself was no adherent of the geomantic superstitions of his time, but it also shows that he had not the spirit to attack and expose the absurdity and futility of a doctrine incompatible with the belief in one supreme and intelligent ruler of the universe. But he never explained clearly whether he held this belief, or whether his God was merely the physical heaven. Nor did his disciples assume a bolder attitude against superstition. They followed the example of their master and observed a studied neutrality, allowing the faith in the personal god of their revered ancient sages to be quietly supplanted by Tauistic speculations among the learned and polytheistic practices among the unlearned. They did not themselves believe in divination, but fully approved the application of the diagrams for purposes of divination. They did not believe in the cosmogonic speculations of their contemporaries, but they expressed no opinion on the question how the world was made. Thus they left the door open for all forms of superstition. No doubt the above-mentioned geomantic ideas spread far and wide under this studied silence of the guardians of ancient wisdom and knowledge, though we have no data as to the extent or progress achieved by that earliest form of Feng-shui during this period. It is reported, however, that about the close of this period (B.C. 249) a scholar, called

Shu-li-tsih, asserted that he had chosen his grave in a situation which would cause it at some future time to be flanked by an imperial palace; in other words, that he had found a place where he would have himself buried after his death, and that the geomantic affinities of that place were such as to cause one of his descendants to gain the throne of China.

The rise of the Han dynasty (B.C. 202) opened a new period in the history of primitive Feng-shui. When the law for the suppression of classical writings was repealed (B.C. 190), and every scrap that had escaped the incendiary mania of the despot of Tsin was eagerly collected, in order to re-publish the ancient classics, a new zest was given to Confucian studies, expounders of the classics multiplied, and Confucianism had another change to re-establish the ancient faith. But again Confuciansim was found wanting. The opening thus afforded, in the awakening of a national interest for literature, and the opportunity given to the expounders of Confucianism to set themselves and their ancient tradition right with the speculations and superstitions of their contemporaries, and to repress the absurdities of Tauist astrologers and alchemysts by popular expositions of the rationale of the ancient faith and further development of it by rational study of nature, this great opening was sacrificed by Confucianists to a pedantic study of the literal meaning of their ancient texts and a dry exposition of the ancient creed. But Tauism availed of the opportunity rejected by Confucianism and raised a literature abounding in the supernatural and the marvellous which filled the minds of the people with astrological and mystic speculations and swelled the tide of superstition so that Confucianists even remain imbued with it to the present day. The very man, whose name is famous for his success in re-editing the lost Confucian classics, Lew-heang (B.C. 40), betrayed by a report he sent to the throne, as a public censor, that he believed in the geomantic superstitions, which, under the influence of Tauist astrology and cosmogony, naturally received a new impetus during this period. He reported to the Emperor, that *nefandum fas*, on the grave of a man called Wong (king), a native of Tsie-nan in Shan-tung, two trees were so inter-twined that even the leaves grew into each other, that the form of the grave resembled an erect stone or a willow whose branches grew upward. He insinuated that these were indications shewing that one of the descendants of this man would become Emperor of China, a broad hint to extinguish the whole family.

It was during this period that the first attempt was made to gather up the popular notions then current among the people concerning geomancy and to form them into a system. The first exponent of this system of Feng-shui is a book, published under the Han dynasty under the title Tseh-king (*lit.* the canon of the dwellings). To give the book the halo of antiquity it was asserted that the ancient Hwang-ti was its author, which assertion, though probably believed in at the time by many, was of course utterly unfounded. Even the catalogues of books published under the Han, Sui and Tang dynasties, which mention the book in question, do not mention Hwang-ti as its author. This book, however, is not only a condensation of the geomantic superstitions of former ages, but it carries the doctrine of Feng-shui farther by extending the geomantic influences, which were formerly ascribed to graves only, to the dwellings of the living. The latter were called "male dwellings"; tombs were styled "female dwellings". It also divided the diagrams, formerly only used for purposes of divination, into male and female diagrams, and applied them to determine the geomantic character of both graves and dwelling houses. Of Wen-wang's eight diagrams those for wind (S.E.), fire (S.), earth (S.W.) and ocean (W.) were said to work in accordance with the female energy of nature, whilst the influence of heaven (N.W.), water (N.) mountains (N.E.) and thunder (E.) was declared to be in accordance with the male principle of creation. The book distinguishes twenty-four different means of averting calamity and insuring prosperity by applying these diagrams according to as many different methods, and the compilers of the Imperial catalogue think there is some good sense in these manipulations with the diagrams of Wen-wang.

The next period in the history of Feng-shui includes the time of the Three Kingdoms (A.D. 221-277) and that of the so-called Six Dynasties (A.D. 265-618). The influence which geomantic ideas obtained at the very beginning of this period is sufficiently illustrated by an incident related in the records of the first of those Three Kingdoms, the so-called Posterior Han dynasty (A.D. 221-263). It is reported, as a matter beyond dispute, that one Yuen-ngan, desirous to find, on the occasion of his occasion of his father's death, a suitable burial ground, went out to look for a place and happened to fall in with three learned men (adepts in the geomantic art), who pointed out a spot which, as they assured him, would secure for his family the highest official distinction and emoluments. He followed their advice, buried his father there, and, strange to say, soon after he was raised to a high office in the state, and his descendants continued for many generations to fill the highest and most remuner-ative posts in the service of the government. In that historical romance called the "Memoirs of the Three Kingdoms" occurs also a passage, which shows that in those early times geomancers had already learned to apply the four quadrants of the starry heavens, the azure dragon in the East, the sable warrior in the North, the white tiger in the West and the vermilion bird in the South, in order to express the varied influences which the twenty-eight constellations were supposed to exercise on the earth. Kwan-lu, it is said, approached the grave of Wu-k'iu-kien and exclaimed, "Behold the white tiger holding a corpse in his mouth, and the vermilion bird dissolved in grief."

This reference to the twenty-eight constellations, which the Chinese, dropping the several names of the Nakchatras, borrowed from Hindoo astronomy, betrays already the rising influence of Buddhism. This foreign religion, officially recognized in China by one of the Han Emperors (A.D. 62), had been propagated for several centuries in different parts of China and slowly gained a foothold. But during the reign of the above-mentioned Six Dynasties, and especially in the course of the Tsin dynasty (A.D. 265-419), Buddhism became a power in the state, and gradually saturated the whole nation with its atheistic and fatalistic ideas. These doctrines naturally stimulated the progress and development of those geomantic vagaries, which had hitherto been wanting a centre and a rational basis on which they might be formed into a system. Buddhism, with its atheism, fatalism and its doctrine of the ceaseless rotation of cosmic destructions and re-constructions (Kalpas), supplied this want. Accordingly we find that Feng-shui received during this period, and especially under the Tsin dynasty, a new impetus, new allies, new expositors. A famous but somewhat mythical personage, Ko-po, is said to have collected all the ancient traditions concerning Feng-shui and published them in a book, still extant, the Tsang-shoo (book of interment), which is to the present day one of the principal sources of references for the student of Feng-shui. Many geomancers call Ko-po the founder of modern Feng-shui, but they have no evidence to show in favour of this assertion beyond the simple fact, recorded in history, that Ko-po was an adept in geomancy and lived under the Tsin dynasty. Even the Tsang-shoo classic itself, which treats Feng-shui with special reference to the forms and outlines of nature, cannot be satisfactorily proved to have been written by Ko-po. For it is not mentioned in the catalogues of the literature produced during this period. The Tsang-shoo is first mentioned in the catalogue of the Tang dynasty (A.D. 618-905); but even here no author is assigned to it, no mention of Ko-po, to whom only the catalogue of the Sung dynasty (A.D. 960-1126) ascribes the authorship of this classic.

Still it remains more than probable that the Feng-shui superstitions received great attention and encouragement under the reign of the Six Dynasties. It is a significant fact that all the imperial annals of these several dynasties contain, among other subjects, separate chapters on felicitous geomantic influences. And history reports as a remarkable circumstance, that Wen-ti, the first Emperor of the Sui dynasty (A.D. 589) considered it worth his while to start an argument against the truth of Feng-shui. When he raised his standard, his enemies desecrated the tombs of his ancestors in order to bring upon him the calamities which Feng-shui teaches to be the natural consequence of a destroyed tomb, but notwithstanding this he succeeded in his endeavour to gain the throne, though he lost a brother on the battle-field. The words put into his mouth by the imperial historiographer of his dynasty are: "If the tombs of my ancestors are not in a felicitous (geomantic) position, why did I attain to the throne? but if their position is felicitous, why was my brother killed?" It was probably in consequence of this imperial dictum, that in after times the expositors of Feng-shui invented subtle theories, to explain how one and the same grave (or dwelling) might cause misfortunes to overtake one and showers of blessings to descend upon another member of the same family.

With the rise of the Tang dynasty (A.D. 618-905), which is famous for its revival of literature generally and of poetical literature especially, which had hundreds of Buddhistic works translated from Sanskrit into Chinese, a new era opened, particuarly favourable to the propagation of mystic and fanciful doctrines assuming, as geomancy had learned to do, the garb of national as well as Tauistic and Buddhistic philosophy. The notion of five planets (Venus, Jupiter, Mercury, Mars, and Saturn) influencing the earth and every living being, made its first appearance about this time, and was eagerly taken told of by the professor of Feng-shui. The above-mentioned "book of interment" became now a popular hand-book, and various other books, among which the Han-lung-king (the canon on the art of rousing the dragon), the Ts'ing-nang-king (the canon of the green bag) and the E-lung-king (the canon on the doubtful dragon), are the most important. The Han-lung-king mentions also, in addition to the five planets, the above-mentioned nine stars, which some commentators refer to the constellation called bushel, whilst others explain them to be the seven stars of the Great Bear with two neighbouring stars, others again declaring them to be floating about in space. But the Han-lung-king bases on the influence of these stars a whole theory of selecting propitious sites for houses or tombs. The Ts'ing-nang-king opens with an exposition of the mystic properties of the combination of even and uneven numbers (1-6, 2-7, 3-8, 4-6, 5-10), and proceeds to lay down the rule, that everything in heaven has its counterpart (in corresponding numbers) on earth. The E-lung-king refers especially to those forms and outlines of nature where dragon and tiger do not prominently stand forth and are as it were concealed. The authorship of these three books is ascribed to Yang-kwan-tsung, who professed to be a disciple of Ko-po and who developed especially that part of the Feng-shui system which refers to the signs of dragon and tiger, to the direction and shape of watersheds and the influence of water-courses.

But it was not till the rise of the Sung dynasty (A.D. 960) that all the above-mentioned elements of the geomantic art gathered into one grand system, built up on a philosophical basis and developed methodically so as to combine every form of influence which heaven may be said to exercise on earth and which both heaven and earth were supposed to have on human affairs. This system is in fact but a practical application of the materialistic speculations for which Chow-leen-k'e, Chang-ming-taou, the two brothers Ch'ing, and most expecially the illustrious Choo-he gained such general acceptation, that their cosmogonic theory of the universe,

their speculations concerning the Great Absolute, the male
and female principles and the two-fold breath of nature as
the prime agents of all physical phenomena, became the
national faith of China. No wonder then the devotees of
Feng-shui, wisely adopting all that was popular and attractive
in this grand scheme of natural philosophy, and promulgat-
ing their fantastic geomantic speculations in accordance with
the favourite terminology of Choo-he, came in for a share in
that national favour and national popularity which the
great philosophers of the Sung dynasty so justly obtained. A
scholar called Wang-k'e was the chief representative of the
Feng-shui profession at this time. He assumed to be a disciple
of Ko-po, and claims the credit of having invented the theory
of the mutual production and destruction of the five
elements (p.18). It was he that systematized, in the phrase-
ology of the new philosophy, all the traditional ideas on
geomancy and reorganized the Feng-shui art on the basis of
Choo-he's materialism.

At the present day the adherents of Feng-shui are divided
into two classes or schools, the Tsung-miau (ancestral temple)
school, which took its rise in Foh-kien, and the Kwang-si
school. In the preceding chapters I have explained the more
prominent theories which these schools have in common, and
I have therefore merely to add, that these two schools are
chiefly distinguished by the comparative prominence each
gives to one or other of four divisions of the Feng-shui
system. The Foh-kien school of geomancers, claiming Wang-
K'e as their founder, attribute the greatest importance to the
doctrines of the order of nature (Li) and of the numerical
proportions of nature (Su). They are therefore specially
attached to the use of the compass. The second school, called
the Kwang-si school of geomancers, because it took its rise in
the Kwang-si province, claim Yang-kwan-tsung as their
founder, and lay the greatest stress on the doctrines of the
breath (K'e) and outlines (Ying) of nature. They use the
compass too, but only as a subordinate help in prospecting

the country, for their principle is, first to look for the visible symptoms of dragon and tiger and of a good breath, and then to judge of the surrounding influences by consulting the compass.

These two schools have produced a very voluminous literature, which is, however, but an expansion of the above-mentioned ideas on the basis of the philosophy of Choo-he.

Having thus traced the history and literature of Feng-shui down to the present, it only remains for me to add a few words as to the extent of influence which this strange medley of superstition, ignorance and philosophy possesses at the present day.

In Feng-shui we have what may be called, from a Chinese point of view, a complete amalgamation of religion and science. Unfortunately, however, the religious element in Feng-shui was through the early disappearing of the ancient theism distorted into a form of gross superstition, half Tauistic, half Buddhistic, and what I have hitherto, by a stretch of charity, called Chinese physical science is, from a scientific point of view, but a conglomeration of rough guesses of nature, sublimated by fanciful play with puerile diagrams.

But however that may be, the fact remains nevertheless, that Feng-shui is at present a power in China. It is an essential part of ancestral worship, which national religion, neither Tauism nor Buddhism managed to deprive of its all-pervading influence. Feng-shui is, moreover, so engrafted upon Chinese social life, it has become so firmly intertwined with every possible event of domestic life (birth, marriage, house-building, funerals, etc.) that it cannot be uprooted without a complete overthrow and consequent re-organisation of all social forms and habits. The pious reverence which every Chinaman accords to whatever can claim the prestige of

The Yellow Pagoda and fort on the Canton River.

antiquity, is another element explaining the wide-spread influence of Feng-shui. Its origin can indeed be traced back, as I have shewn, to remote ages, but popular opinion connects the origin of Feng-shui with the ancient Hwang-ti, and looks upon this system as being as ancient as China itself. Another consideration gains for Feng-shui the respect and sympathy even of many educated and learned men. This is the fundamental connection in which Feng-shui boasts to stand with the scheme of diagrams, as laid down in the Yih-king, and the fact that the whole system of Feng-shui is in perfect unity with the vagaries of Tauists and Buddhists on the one hand and Choo-he's modern philosophy on the other. Feng-shui is indeed the refined quintessence of Tauistic mysticism, Buddhistic fatalism and Choo-he's materialism, and as such it commands if not the distinct approval yet the secret sympathy of every Chinaman, high or low.

Of course highly educated and particularly intelligent Confucianists will not acknowledge that they believe in the crude apocalyptic utterances of an ordinary geomancer, but within their own walls these same intellectual Confucianists will after all regulate every single domestic affair in strict accordance with the most approved canons of Feng-shui. Of course the Chinese Government, as such, will not acknowledge the catholicity and orthodoxy of Feng-shui, and yet it publishes year after year, with expressedly Imperial sanction, an almanac containing all the tables and data, references and diagrams, that a geomancer requires as a daily vade mecum.

Feng-shui has a legal status in China. When there is any-where in China a dispute between people on the ground of alleged interference with and disturbance of the Feng-shui aspects of a grave or house, the judicial tribunals of China will entertain the claim, examine into its merits and decide the case on the presumption that Feng-shui is a reality and a truth, not a fiction. Feng-shui has even a political status in China. When a rebellion breaks out in any of the eighteen provinces, the first step invariably taken by the Government is not to raise troops, but to dispatch messengers instructed to find out the ancestral tombs of the several leaders of the rebellion, to open the tombs, scatter their contents and desecrate the graves in all possible ways. For this is supposed to be the surest means of injuring the prospects and marring the possible success of the rebels. Again, when land had to be ceded to the hated foreigner up and down the China Coast, as a so-called foreign concession, the Chinese Government would invariable select a spot condemned by the best experts in Feng-shui as one that combined a deadly breath with all those indications of the compass which imply dire calamities upon all that settle down there and their children's children. If the spot had not to be ceded by treaty, it would be pointed out to the unsuspecting foreigner as the only one open for sale, and anyhow the ignorant barbarian sceptic would become the supposed dupe and laughing-stock of the astute Chinaman.

Witness, for instance the views held by intelligent Chinese with regard to the island of Sha-meen, the foreign concession, so to say, of Canton. It was originally a mud flat in the Canton river in the very worst position Feng-shui knows of. It was conceded to the imperious demand of the foreign powers as the best available place of residence for foreigners, and when it was found that the Canton trade, once so prodigious, would not revive, would not flourish there, in spite of all the efforts of its supporters—when it was discovered that every house built on Sha-meen was overrun as soon as built with white ants, boldly defying coal tar, carbolic acid and all other foreign appliances—when it was noticed that the English Consul, though having a special residence built for him there, would rather live two miles off in the protecting shadow of a Pagoda—it was a clear triumph of Feng-shui and of Chinese statemanship.

Powerful, however, as Feng-shui is, it is by no means an

insuperable barrier to the introduction of foreign civilisation in China. For it possesses an extraordinary amount of flexibility. It may be turned and twisted by skilful manipulation to suit almost any combination of circumstances. The most calamitous formation of country, the most portentous accumulation of deadly breath or ill-starred influences can be rectified by skill and unsparing exertion, so that all evil influences are either fended off or turned into instruments of blessing. Money, therefore, will go a long way to remove obstacles or collisions with Feng-shui. But it is a dangerous weapon, and will, if once employed, call forth an endless array of claims for money to compensate Feng-shui damages.

The only powerful agent likely to overthrow the almost universal reign of Feng-shui in China I conceive to be the spread of sound views of natural science,the distribution of useful knowledge in China. There is one truth in Feng-shui, on which both this Chinese system of natural science and our Western views of physics are based. It is the recognition of the uniformity and universality of the operation of natural laws. There is one great defect in Feng-shui, which our Western physicists have happily long ago discarded. This is the neglect of an experimental but at the same time critical survey of nature in all its details. Let this defect be supplied by a full and popular exposition of the afore-mentioned uniformity and universality of the laws of nature; let correct views be spread regarding those continually interchanging forces of nature, heat, electricity, magnetism, chemical affinity and motion, let these views be set forth in as forcible and attractive but popular a form as Choo-he employed, and the issue of the whole cannot be doubtful. The fires of science will purge away the geomantic dross, but only that the truth may shine forth in its golden glory.

I began with the question: what is Feng-shui? I may properly conclude by putting the same question again. What is Feng-shui? My readers will probably agree with me in the remark that Feng-shui is the foolish daughter of a wise mother. It starts with a few notions of astronomy or rather astrology, hazy and obscure, but respectable enough, considering that it was more than two thousand years ago that the Chinese took hold of them. It is based on a materialistic scheme of philosophy, which had studied nature, in a pious and reverential yet in a very superficial and grossly superstitious manner, but which trusting in the force of a new logical formulæ and mystic diagrams, endeavoured to solve all the problems of nature and to explain everything in heaven above and on the earth below with some mathematical categories. The result, of course, is a farrago of nonsense and childish absurdities.

The whole system of Feng-shui may contain a bushel of wisdom, but it scarcely contains a handful of common sense. What is Feng-shui, then? It is simply the blind gropings of the Chinese mind after a system of natural science, which gropings, untutored by practical observation of nature and trusting almost exclusively in the truth of alleged ancient tradition and in the force of abstract reasoning, naturally left the Chinese mind completely in the dark. The system of Feng-shui, therefore, based as it is on human speculation and superstition and not on careful study of nature, is marked for decay and dissolution; for, as Wordsworth said—

To the solid ground
Of Nature trusts the mind that builds for aye.

FINIS

AFTERWORD

Feng-shui and its future.

The author's closing remarks, about feng-shui being a mere superstition, a relic of the child-like mentality of the past and so on, were surely added so as to make his book more acceptable to his religious superiors and perhaps to his publishers. As a missionary he was, after all, supposed to be engaged in reforming the Chinese outlook and impressing upon it the stamp of Christianity and modern European rationalism. Few of his generation had any doubt that the philosophy of science and the religion of the dominant western civilizations must eventually prevail over all other traditions and modes of thought, and the common conviction was that native practices such as feng-shui were destined for early oblivion. It was impossible for Eitel to be unaffected by that notion; his professional duty indeed was to uphold it, and a particularly interesting feature of his book is his evident waverings between loyalty to his mission and the respect he had developed for the subtle philosophy and natural sciences of old China. Typical of the latter is his outburst (page 5):

"Yet I say, would God, that our own men of science had preserved in their observatories, laboratories and lecture-

Gardens of the Imperial Palace, Peking.

rooms that same child-like reverence for the living powers of nature, that sacred awe and trembling fear of the mysteries of the unseen, that firm belief in the reality of the invisible world and its constant intercommunication with the seen and the temporal, which characterise these Chinese gropings after natural science."

That was written by the same man who, later in the same book, could speak of feng-shui as a product of "human speculation and superstition and not on careful study of nature"!

The nineteenth-century writers who introduced the concept of feng-shui to the West were mostly China Missionaries, beginning with the Rev. Yates who wrote the first English article on the subject in 1868. Eitel's was the only western book on feng-shui up to recent times, and his account was long unrivalled other than by that of J.J.M. de Groot, a Dutch colonial administrator, in his monumental *Religious System of China*. Not until the 1950s, when Joseph Needham began publishing the volumes of his great work, *Science and Civilization in China*, revealing to what advantage the Chinese had developed their traditional sciences, was it possible for western readers to appreciate the scientific context in which feng-shui flourished. Interest in the subject has been growing ever since, and modern writers on feng-shui no longer feel required, as Eitel did, to apologize for taking it seriously or, like de Groot, to refer to it as 'quasi-science'. In fact, the tables have been well and truly turned, and the Chinese 'natural science' which Eitel believed and half-feared to be on the verge of extinction is now becoming recognized as a model for the reformed code of science which the circumstances of our time are demanding.

With the demise of imperial China early this century feng-shui lost its official status and its exponents reverted to private practice. Most educated Chinese by that time no longer professed to believe in it, though its influence remained strong among the people. It also began spreading.

Emigrant Chinese populations, throughout Asia and on the west coast of America, took feng-shui with them. Its practitioners soon adapted their art to local circumstances, and the notorious aptitude of the Chinese to prosper abroad was credited by them to the skill of their feng-shui men. This phenomenon began to attract attention from the natives. In California particularly, where the old-established, powerful Chinese colonies had long set the standards of civilization, the influence of feng-shui has spread beyond the Asian community to affect other cultures. The early 1970s the writer of this note had the benefit of meeting Dr Wong, a feng-shui man of Mill Valley near San Francisco, who maintained a flourishing practice among the Californian locals. His clients were mostly young people, looking for a more practical form of guidance than could be obtained from the generalized wisdom of Hindu sages, and this Dr Wong provided, applying his art to weighty problems of money and romance as well as to the details of where they should place their kitchens, how their beds should be orientated and on which days it would be best to avoid going out of the house.

As a youth in China Dr Wong had been apprenticed to a local feng-shui man and had learnt his craft in the field, following his teacher on daily walks about the countryside (carrying the old man's water-bottle and umbrella) and training his eye to perceive the paths of dragon and tiger and the flow of vital currents in the landscape features. A modern education diverted him into western medicine and the habits of thought that go with it. In retirement in California his appearance and manner were those of a modern European. By then, however, his interest in feng-shui, dutifully forgotten during the course of his career, had been renewed; and for that Dr Wong gave a typically down-to-earth, practical reason: that it worked. Why it should do so he had no idea, but that did not worry him. In his feng-shui consulting-rooms he dealt with clients' problems, real and imagined, and charged the proper fee like any other good professional man.

This aspect of its function, as a code for regulating daily life and acquiring prosperity, has mainly been the cause of popular interest in feng-shui today. Most normal people are interested in how to succeed in life, and that is the type of advice in which modern feng-shui men specialize. Though officially forbidden in mainland China, feng-shui has a strong hold in Hong Kong and among Chinese colonies overseas. Its influences indeed appears to be growing. Chinese businessmen, brought up to despise feng-shui as a part of outmoded tradition, are no longer ashamed, as their fathers might have been, to admit its efficacy and take advantage of it. In areas with large Chinese populations it is now the custom for planning authorities and business corporations to take feng-shui advice on the designing of public works and office buildings. Thus they avoid the expensive alterations which would be necessary if their finished constructions offended local feng-shui susceptibilities.

In China itself feng-shui was officially outlawed at the communist Revolution as being an affront to the Marxist faith in 'scientific atheism'. Since then, however, traditional Chinese culture has been assertive in regaining state recognition, and in several areas it has succeeded. This is notably the case with traditional medicine and acupuncture, which is based on the same principles as feng-shui, being concerned with the flow of subtle energies in the human body which correspond to those perceived by feng-shui in the body of the earth. Acupuncture and feng-shui have been described as two departments of the same science. The one having returned to favour, the other is no doubt quietly following, though with new associations and imagery. According to a report from China a few years ago, rock formations at a famous resort, which were named after their resemblances to various mythological characters and symbols, had been officially declared to resemble certain heroic characters or episodes of the Revolution, and had been renamed accordingly. Another recent anecdote, showing that Chinese scientists have not been deprived of their humour and sense of tradition, comes from a remote country district. A certain village caught the scientists' attention because of the abnormal number of twins being born there. They descended on the villagers, subjected them to tests and analyzed the local soil, water and whatever else might imaginably be the cause of the phenomenon. But no features were discovered which were different from those of neighbouring villages where the incidence of twins was normal. Finally, in despair, the scientists took the unscientific step of questioning the villagers themselves about the cause of their abnormal propensity. The first local they approached, an old woman, immediately solved the problem by pointing to a nearby mountain, invisible from the other villages, which was in the form of twin peaks.

In similar vein our friend Wong attributes the romantic disposition of Mill Valley girls to the influence of their dominant mountain, Tamalpais, which is shaped like a recumbant Indian maiden, a character of local legend. The notion that natural shapes in the landscape tend to affect the characters and destinies of those living within sight of them gave rise to one of the two main branches of feng-shui, the Earthly Forms school which Eitel describes. The other school, the cosmological, paid more attention to astronomical factors, horoscopes and readings of the geomancer's compass. Neither of these branches necessarily originated in China, and the Chinese claim no monopoly of feng-shui, saying that once it was practised world-wide. There is much evidence of this being true. Native cultures in Africa, America and many parts of Asia retain various local codes of feng-shui, while megalithic monuments in Europe, Stonehenge included, have symbolic astronomical features and significant legends which suggest that their original function was in connection with feng-shui practice in prehistoric antiquity. The existence of an Earthly Forms school in ancient Greece is evidenced by the photographs in Vincent Scully's *The*

Earth, the Temple and the Gods, showing how shrines and temples in the archaic Greek landscape were sited in relation to symbolic shapes in the local mountains. These become apparent under certain conditions of light and shadow, and Scully suggests that such moments coincided with stages in the temple rituals when the god being celebrated would be seen to appear in the distance as a natural rock effigy. In Australia the Aborigines' sacred places are often marked by a rock outcrop roughly resembling a certain type of creature. Such places may be noted as the generation centres of the animal depicted and as locations of events involving that species in the local creation myth. In that primeval mode of perception, exercised by every healthy dreamer, is the origin of the poetic Earthly Forms school of feng-shui.

The Australian variety of feng-shui is a topical subject. The Aborigines have preserved a more pristine culture than the Chinese, and their tradition is nearer to its roots. From the way they regard their mythological landscape there is much to be learnt about the origins and essential nature of feng-shui as practised elsewhere. Their situation today is like that of the nineteenth-century Chinese, confronted with an alien economic power which denies recognition to the vital spirit in land and feels justified in exploiting it for temporary material profit. The Aborigines, to whom every detail of their land has ritual and cosmological significance, react as the Chinese did with incomprehension and anger to schemes for laying waste to it, such as are regularly proposed by industrial and mining concerns. It is obvious who the usual winner is in these disputes, but the Aborigines are skillful negotiators and are practised at compromising with developers and road-planning authorities so as to avert the most disastrous of the threats to their sanctuaries and the feng-shui of their country.

The use of feng-shui for attracting good fortune to individuals and business companies may, as suggested above, be the most popular cause of its revival today. The deeper cause, however, is the former universal acceptance — and thus the potential future acceptance — of a science which is so obviously relevant to the present, an ecological science which studies the best interests of the earth itself together with all its life-forms, human nature included. Feng-shui was responsible for the condition which has often been remarked on by travellers in China, that the countryside looked like a beautifully landscaped park, studded with temples, pagodas, grottoes and other impractical objects, yet supporting a large, contented population. The modern assumption is that these two features are incompatible, that people are natural despoilers of the landscape and that the best one can hope for is to preserve certain areas of natural beauty for rest and recreation, while sacrificing others to 'progress'. Feng-shui has a different aim: to harmonize human interests with those of the earth and its other creatures, allowing each district to reflect, as far as possible, the ideal image of this earth as our natural paradise.

Feng-shui offers a principled but highly flexible code which can be referred to over all matters of architectural design, city planning and the use of the countryside. These subjects today are governed by a variety of different authorities, each with their own, temporarily fashionable theories but with no scientific standards on which to base their decisions. The result is apparent in the chaotic appearance of any modern city and the country surrounding it, in the wasteful use of land and the ugliness and inefficiency of modern environments. These evils can at least be mitigated by adopting some of the basic, humane principles of feng-shui, the first of which is that the earth is best regarded as an actual living creature, whose health, condition and spirit are reflected in all the other creatures dependent on it. This simple view, which was universally accepted up to quite recent times, produces results from the very beginning. For one thing, it sets a standard of judgement in disputes between native populations and representatives of economic progress, allowing both sides to express their interests on equal terms.

It serves also to rationalize the activities of conservationists and 'friends of the earth' groups who, for all their fine spirit, are constantly disadvantaged by having to base their appeals on emotion or aesthetics for lack of a coherent alternative world-view to set against the one now in force.

The concept of a living earth, whose vital energies are related to those of our own bodies, introduces the need for a new approach to science which is more in keeping with this state of affairs. As a candidate for fulfilling this need, feng-shui has an impressive record of achievements, the most notable being the sanctified but functional landscape of old China. The ways and techniques of feng-shui can be studied through Eitel and other authors, but more essential is the cosmology or general attitude to life which engendered feng-shui and which is ultimately inseparable from its practice. Human inventiveness is such that, once the need for a reformed code of science is widely or officially acknowledged, the secrets of the earth's energies and the methods of feng-shui in relation to it could be rediscovered, in terms appropriate to the present. That type of science is incompatible with many of the dominant institutions of today, with many of the assumptions behind modern economics and with fantastic notions about space colonies and exploitations of other worlds. Feng-shui answers other requirements, those which arise naturally in human society. It was designed to allow the greatest possible number of people on earth to enjoy full lives of happiness and security by studying the interests of nature and adapting their ways accordingly.

In answer to Eitel's repeated query, What is feng-shui?, the following is suggested: The art of perceiving the subtle energies that animate nature and the landscape, and the science of reconciling the best interests of the living earth with those of all its inhabitants.

John Michell

CONCISE BIBLIOGRAPHY ON FENG-SHUI

Ball, J. Dyer, *Things Chinese*. London, 1904

Börschmann, E. *Picturesque China*. T. Fisher Unwin, London, 1924

Edkins, J. 'Feng-shui', in *Chinese Recorder and Missionary Journal*, March 1872

Feuchtwang, S.D.R. *An Anthropological Analysis of Chinese Geomancy*. Vithagna, Laos, 1974

de Groot, J.J.M. *The Religious System of China*. Vol.3, pp. 935-1056. Leiden, 1897

Johnston, R.F. *Lion and Dragon in Northern China*. London, 1910

Lip, E. *Chinese Geomancy*. Times Books, Singapore, 1979

Lip Mong Har. *Geomancy, Building, Development and Construction*. Singapore, 1977

Michell, J. *The Earth Spirit*. Thames & Hudson, London, 1975
Simulacra. Thames & Hudson, London, 1979

Needham, J. *Science and Civilization in China,* vols 2, 3 and 4:1. Cambridge University Press, 1956-62

Pennick, N. *The Ancient Science of Geomancy*. Thames & Hudson, London, 1979

Porter, L.L. 'Feng-shui, or how the Chinese keep in tune with Nature', in *Chinese Recorder and Missionary Journal,* December 1920

Roberts, A. *Geomancy, a Synthonal Reappraisal.* Zodiac House, Somerset, 1981

Rossbach, S. *Feng Shui: the Chinese Art of Placement.* Hutchinson, London, 1984

Skinner, S. *The Living Earth Manual of Feng-Shui.* Routledge & Kegan Paul, London, 1982

Yates, M. 'Ancestral Worship and Feng-shui', in *Chinese Recorder and Missionary Journal,* vol. 1, 1868

THE LIVING EARTH MANUAL OF FENG-SHUI

Stephen Skinner

The Living Earth Manual of Feng-Shui by Stephen Skinner is available in a low-priced Asian Edition first published in 1983 by Graham Brash (Pte) Ltd, Singapore.

The book provides a basic outline of the art of feng-shui — its history, principles and application. It describes how this ancient Chinese art has formed the basis of man's relationship with nature in the East for many hundreds of years, providing the means of living in harmony with the land and deriving the greatest benefit, peace and prosperity from being in the right place at the right time. The rules of feng-shui apply equally to the siting and arrangement of cities, offices, houses, tombs, and even flats and bedsits. The feng-shui practicioner tracks the hidden flow of energy (ch'i) which runs through the land in dragon-lines similar to the acupuncture meridians of the body. In this book the science of 'riding the dragon' is laid out in an easily accessible manner.

Stephen Skinner graduated from Sydney University and lectured in geography before migrating to the United Kingdom in 1972 to further his research into magical manuscripts in the British Museum. It was here that he became interested in geomancy and feng-shui. A recent trip to the East has put him in touch with modern practicioners of feng-shui, especially in Hong Kong and Singapore where feng-shui experts are consulted by even the largest and most modern building companies on projects ranging from new towns to high-rise office and residential blocks.

FUN WITH ASTROLOGY, Evelyn Lip — same format as above, but this book deals with the Western signs of the zodiac.

GOLDEN LOTUS Books 1–4, trans. Clement Egerton — an English edition of the Chinese classic *Chin P'ing Mei*.

INTRODUCTION TO TAI CHI, Gary Khor — teaches the basic movements in Tai Chi. Well illustrated with helpful photographs.

MYTHS & LEGENDS OF CHINA, E.T.C. Werner — a comprehensive and in-depth study of Chinese mythology, illustrated with 32 beautiful colour plates.

OLD TALES OF CHINA, Li Nianpei — interesting information on the mythological and historical names and stories frequently encountered in Chinese art and literature.

SAYINGS OF CONFUCIUS, compiled by Peter Burgess — covers a wide range of subjects from the status of women to the government of a country. Illustrated with small, amusing sketches.

SELECTED QUOTATIONS FROM THE EAST AND WEST, compiled by Peter Burgess — famous and unknown, past and present, Oriental and Occidental are comprehensively covered. Quotations arranged according to themes.

SHORT STORIES OF THE FAR EAST — an anthology of the best known Far Eastern stories by such favourite authors as Somerset Maugham, Pearl Buck, etc.

BRASH BOOKS BOOK CLUB
GRAHAM BRASH (PTE) LTD
HEAD OFFICE, SALES & WAREHOUSE
32 GUL DRIVE, SINGAPORE 2262.
TEL: 8611336, 8620437
TELEX: RS 23718 FEENIX GB
FAX: 65-8614815

We hope that you have enjoyed reading this book by **Graham Brash**. It is one in a list of over 600 publications covering a wide range of subject areas. To find out more about related titles, you can join our book club today.

BRASH BOOKS is a specialised book club which selects publications for its members according to their reading interests. Membership is free and book information, special discounts and other benefits (invitations to book-signings, for example) are mailed to members regularly.

To join **BRASH BOOKS** , simply complete this form and either fax or mail it to the above address. Upon receipt, a free catalogue will be forwarded to you. Thank you for becoming a **BRASH BOOK** reader.

Name: ....
Tel/Fax: ....
Address: ....
Date of Birth : ....
....
Occupation: ....
....
Marital Status: ....

Area(s) of Interest:

( ) Asian Interest
( ) Asian Literature
( ) Mind, Body, Spirit
( ) Business/Management/
Self-Improvement
( ) Fiction – Adult
( ) Fiction – Children
( ) Education/Study
( ) General Interest

( ) Others (please specify):
1) ....
2) ....
3) ....
Languages:
( ) German
( ) French
( ) Others (please specify):
....